ROSEMARY CONLEY'S
HIP AND THIGH DIET
& COOKBOOK

By Rosemary Conley:

Rosemary Conley's Hip and Thigh Diet (Arrow Books)
Rosemary Conley's *Complete* Hip and Thigh Diet (Arrow Books)

ROSEMARY CONLEY'S

HIP AND THIGH DIET
& COOKBOOK

Rosemary Conley & Patricia Bourne

CENTURY
London   Sydney   Auckland   Johannesburg

First published in 1989 by Century Hutchinson Ltd,
Brookmount House, 62–65 Chandos Place, Covent Garden,
London WC2N 4NW

Century Hutchinson Australia Pty Ltd, 89–91 Albion Street,
Surry Hills, Sydney, New South Wales 2010, Australia

Century Hutchinson New Zealand Ltd, PO Box 40-086,
Glenfield, Auckland 10, New Zealand

Century Hutchinson South Africa (Pty) Ltd, PO Box 337,
Bergvlei, 2012 South Africa

Designed by Sue Storey
Photographs by Patrick McLeavey and Sue Storey

Set in Linotron 202 Gill by
Rowland Phototypesetting Ltd, Bury St Edmunds, Suffolk

Printed by OFSA S.p.a., (Casarile), Milan, Italy

British Library Cataloguing in Publication Data

Conley, Rosemary 1946–
    Rosemary Conley's hip and thigh diet & cookbook
    1. Food: Low fat dishes – recipes
    I. Title.   II. Bourne, Patricia 1927–
    641.5'638

    ISBN 0-7126-3017-1
    ISBN 0-7126-3539-4 (export paperback)

CONTENTS

ACKNOWLEDGEMENTS

Primarily, I must thank Rosemary, not only for her enthusiastic response to my suggestion for this book but also for introducing me to such a healthy diet which has enabled me after years of trying to lose weight, to do so successfully and with no sense of deprivation. I have thoroughly enjoyed writing this book and I hope that my association with Rosemary will continue.

I also want to thank the ladies from Rosemary's slimming and exercise clubs who so willingly tested recipes for me and sent back their comments (and photographs) which were so useful.

Editors rarely get any acknowledgement and it is only the author who knows how much they have contributed to the presentation of a book. Valerie Buckingham and Kelly Davis have been my editors and I would like to thank them for all their help and advice.

It is often said that in this life, it is whom you know and not what you know that is important. This is particularly true when researching material for a book and I do thank my good friends Kathleen Newton, Tom Cook and Dave Marriott for the time and help they gave me in searching out information which, although it might not be apparent to the reader, is essential to the background of many of these recipes.

Last but not least, I want to thank my husband Tony, in this our Fortieth Anniversary Year, for all the help, support and tenderness he has given me, not only whilst I have been writing this book but throughout all our years together.

Pat Bourne
March 1989

INTRODUCTION

For many, the Hip and Thigh Diet has changed the eating habits of a lifetime and achieved success in reshaping the male and female form far beyond their greatest expectations. Now the *Hip and Thigh Diet & Cookbook* widens the horizon still further for those who are trying to shed successfully those unwanted pounds and inches, as well as offering a wonderful selection of exceptionally tasty dishes. Those who have already enjoyed success in reducing their weight and inches will find the *Hip and Thigh Diet & Cookbook* a real friend in helping them to maintain their new, slimline figures.

Patricia Bourne wrote to me after shedding 1 ½ stones on the Hip and Thigh Diet and suggested we wrote a *Hip and Thigh Diet & Cookbook*. Pat explained that as a professional cook she suffered from the obvious occupational hazard, namely that of being very overweight. I was delighted to hear that Pat had been able to lose weight so easily on my diet and as we worked together in the formation of this book her weight continued to reduce.

The idea of a *Hip and Thigh Diet & Cookbook* had also been suggested by many slimmers who had written to tell me of their wonderful success in losing weight since following the diet. However, my experimental cookery is somewhat restricted – mainly due to lack of time – and in fact my husband, Mike, has become a far more accomplished cook than ever I was, so the thought of writing a comprehensive and interesting cookbook regrettably stayed at the bottom of my list of future projects.

But when Pat Bourne made the suggestion that we should co-write a cookbook, I jumped at the opportunity. She is a qualified chef and, having spent twelve years teaching at the Tante Marie School of Cookery and collaborating on the *Tante Marie Book of Traditional French Cookery*, Pat was appointed Principal of the Tante Marie School after the sudden death of its previous Principal until it was sold. Pat then decided to pursue her writing career and had several books published by Marks & Spencer, and wrote *French Vegetable Cookery* which was published by Macdonald. No one could be better equipped to write the *Hip and Thigh Diet & Cookbook*.

I warmed to Pat instantly when I first met her in London to discuss the possibility of working together on this book. Her synopsis of the cookbook looked deliciously varied and it opened up the Hip and Thigh Diet far beyond the usual restrictions of diet cookery and there are no calories or units to count. What a pleasant change to be looking at ingredients *without* the accompanying list of calorie values so often seen in a diet recipe book. In fact I've never seen a book look less like a diet cookbook. Many of the recipes were tested by members of my slimming and exercise classes who enthused at their originality, ease of preparation and delicious taste. Never has dieting looked so appetising or tasted so exciting.

The recipes have been cleverly designed to incorporate high nutrition, but low fat content. Some will appeal to the experienced cook and others to those who take little delight in spending hours in the kitchen. You can choose from a range of menus that include everyday foods to the more exotic dishes better suited for a special dinner party. How gratifying to be able to entertain guests to a really special menu without giving them the slightest hint that you are on a diet!

Wine and cider have been used for added moisture and extra flavour and there are imaginative menus for vegetarians too.

So how does the Hip and Thigh Diet work?

My very low-fat eating plan was designed in an attempt to avoid surgery for gallstones. Not only did it effectively prevent surgery, but it had the unexpected side-effect of removing inches from my hips and thighs – inches that have caused me considerable embarrassment for years! I tested the low-fat diet on a team of volunteers recruited through local radio to further prove its effectiveness. Based on the staggering results enjoyed by my trial team, my *Hip and Thigh Diet* was published in 1988.

The book shot to number one in the Bestsellers List and stayed there for over six months. I received hundreds of letters from delighted slimmers extolling the virtues of the diet – not only reporting their staggering inch losses, but also significant benefits to their health. It was these comments and revelations that prompted me to extend the diet to cater for an even wider range of tastes, and a follow-up book the *Complete Hip and Thigh Diet* (Arrow) was published earlier this year, and has proved even more successful than the first — selling over half a million copies in the three months following publication.

The principle of the diet is to eliminate all visible fat and reduce to a minimum the intake of those foods which look quite innocent but in fact harbour a surprisingly high amount of fat. Ounce for ounce, fat contains twice as many calories as carbohydrates. Excess fat in our diet deposits itself as fat on the body, whereas carbohydrates burn clean. It is therefore obvious that the best way to reduce the fat in our bodies is to cut down the fat we consume.

Because there is so little fat in this diet it is unnecessary to count calories as, by its very nature, it cuts down on the highest calorie foods. The only way to lose weight is to consume fewer calories than your body needs — losing weight has never been simpler.

For those wishing to lose weight and inches on a serious slimming campaign, I suggest you follow the diet described in the *Complete Hip and Thigh Diet* as it is important to follow and understand fully the instructions given. The *Hip and Thigh Diet & Cookbook* offers a wider variety of low fat dishes for both the Hip and Thigh Dieter and those on the Maintenance Programme.

The diet described in the following pages is based on the original diet followed by my initial trial team, amended to cater for the discerning tastes of those who followed it, and now further extended to incorporate most of the delicious recipes in this cookbook.

The result is an amazing variety of ideas from which you may choose the perfect menu to suit you and your lifestyle. Whether you enjoy the challenge of cookery or prefer to keep it simple, whether you have a vast appetite or a tiny one, there are plenty of recipes from which to choose.

I have included a list of strictly forbidden foods within this section. Before you embark on the diet I must ask you to make a definite resolution that you are not going to eat these forbidden foods. If you are going to cheat, what is the point of going to all the trouble of preparing the delicious dishes in this book? If you are going to sneak bars of chocolate or packets of peanuts when nobody's looking, you might as well not bother with the diet. It has been *proved* that this diet works. It will help you to achieve the kind of figure you never dreamed possible, but there is only one person in the world who can actually make it happen – and that is you!

Perhaps the best news for slimmers is that this diet gives you a greater volume of food than any other reducing diet, and also gives you lots of freedom of choice. You can enjoy three good meals, including a three-course dinner, every single day plus a couple of alcoholic drinks into the bargain.

The choice of menus on the Hip and Thigh Diet has never been as great as is now given within this cookbook. All the main courses have been listed here within the diet and, in addition, you have the opportunity to serve them with vegetables cooked in imaginative and delicious ways.

Following the Hip and Thigh Diet is a most enjoyable way to lose weight and you will be staggered by how quickly you will see results, both in weight and inch loss, and this will encourage you to continue. The additional energy and generally healthier feeling that was experienced by so many of those who wrote to me after following the diet showed they were both surprised and excited by the significant effects of the diet.

Remember also, that the more energy we have, the more energy we are likely to spend in physical activities. And the more physically active we are, the easier it is to lose weight.

Have a great time!

Rosemary Conley

THE HIP AND THIGH DIET

HOW TO USE THE HIP AND THIGH DIET & COOKBOOK

The recipes given can be used to create a three-course dinner menu or taken as individual dishes to comprise a snack lunch or main course. Instructions have been given where necessary to explain which dishes are best suited to those on the Maintenance Programme (e.g. some hors-d'oeuvre) whereas Dieters may eat them for snack lunches.

Pat Bourne has ingeniously created recipes which overcome the limitations of a very low-fat diet. For instance, she has discovered a way of cooking chips by using a tiny amount of fat. Her use of fat-free fromage frais and yogurt has enabled those dishes normally associated with cream or cream cheese to be included. She has maximised the use of those foods which are low in fat and devised ways of whetting every appetite.

Her culinary expertise and techniques are clearly illustrated and explained within this book and I feel certain you will learn a great deal more than just how to prepare low-fat recipes.

Daily allowance
10 fl. oz (250 ml) (½ pint) skimmed low-fat milk or 8 oz (200 ml) semi-skimmed milk, 2 alcoholic drinks (optional)

Diet notes
'Unlimited vegetables' includes potatoes as well as all other vegetables providing they are cooked and served without fat. Pasta, providing it is egg-free and fat-free, may be substituted for potatoes, rice or similar carbohydrate food.

'One piece of fruit' means one average apple or one orange, etc., or approximately 4 oz (100 g) in weight, e.g. a 4 oz (100 g) slice of pineapple.

Red meat: Don't forget to restrict red meat to just two helpings a week.

Thin gravy may be taken with dinner menus providing it is made with gravy powder, not granules. Do not add meat juices from the roasting tin since these contain fat.

All yogurts should be the low-calorie, low-fat, diet brands. Cottage cheese should be the low-fat variety.

Jacket potatoes are stated without a weight restriction. Use your own discretion in order to satisfy your appetite.

Between-meal snacks
Chopped cucumber, celery, carrots, tomatoes and peppers may be consumed between meals if necessary.

PART 1: BREAKFASTS
Select any one of the following:

Cereal breakfasts
The following may be served with skimmed milk from allowance and 1 teaspoon brown sugar if desired.
1. 1 oz (25 g) porridge oats, made with water, served with 2 teaspoons of honey, no sugar.
2. Home-made muesli (made by mixing together ½ oz oats, ½ oz sultanas and ½ banana, 2 teaspoons bran, 1 grated eating apple and 3 oz natural yogurt).
3. 1 oz (25 g) bran flakes or bran flakes with sultanas.
4. 1 oz (25 g) cornflakes, puffed rice, sugar flakes or rye and raisin cereal.
5. 2 Weetabix.
6. 1 oz (25 g) wholewheat cereal.

Fruit breakfasts
N.B. 'Diet yogurt' means low-fat, low-calorie yogurt.
1. 1 banana plus 5 oz (150 g) diet yogurt – any flavour.
2. 4 oz (100 g) tinned peaches in natural fruit juice plus 5 oz (150 g) diet yogurt – any flavour.
3. 5 prunes in natural juice plus 5 oz (150 g) natural diet yogurt.
4. 5 prunes in natural juice plus half a slice of toast plus 1 teaspoon marmalade.
5. 4 dried apricots, soaked overnight in tea, plus 5 oz (150 g) diet yogurt – any flavour.
6. As much fruit as you can eat at one sitting.

7. 5 oz (150 g) stewed fruit (cooked without sugar) plus diet yogurt – any flavour.
8. 6 oz (175 g) fruit compote (e.g. oranges, grapefruit, peaches, pineapple, pears – all in natural juice).
9. 8 oz (225 g) tinned grapefruit in natural juice.
10. 1 whole fresh grapefruit plus 5 oz (150 g) diet yogurt – any flavour.
11. Prunes in Orange Pekoe Tea (see page 100).
12. Spiced Plums (see page 101).

Cooked and continental breakfasts
1. 8 oz (225 g) baked beans served on 1 slice (1 oz) (25 g) toast.
2. 8 oz (225 g) tinned tomatoes served on 1 slice (1 oz) (25 g) toast.
3. 2 oz (50 g) very lean bacon (all fat removed) served with unlimited tinned tomatoes.
4. Half a grapefruit, plus 1 slice (1 oz) (25 g) toast with 2 teaspoons marmalade.
5. 8 oz (225 g) smoked haddock, steamed in skimmed milk.
6. 2 oz (50 g) lean ham, 2 tomatoes, plus 1 fresh wholemeal roll.
7. 2 oz (50 g) cured chicken or turkey breast, 2 tomatoes, plus 1 fresh wholemeal roll.
8. 2 oz (50 g) smoked turkey breast, plus 1 fresh wholemeal roll.
9. 1 oz (25 g) very lean bacon (all fat removed) served with 4 oz (100 g) mushrooms cooked in vegetable stock, 3 oz (75 g) baked beans, 8 oz (225 g) tinned tomatoes or 4 fresh tomatoes grilled.
10. 1 oz (25 g) very lean bacon (all fat removed), 4 oz (100 g) tomatoes or 4 fresh tomatoes grilled, plus half a slice (¾ oz) (18 g) toast.

PART 2: LUNCHES
Select any one of the following:

Fruit lunches
1. 4–5 pieces any fruit (e.g. 1 orange, 1 apple, 1 pear, 4 oz (100 g) plums).
2. 8 oz (225 g) fresh fruit salad topped with 5 oz (150 g) low-fat yogurt.
3. 2 pieces any fresh fruit plus 2 × 5 oz (2 × 150 g) diet yogurts.
4. Chicory and Orange Salad (see page 31).

Packed lunches

1. 2 slices of bread, spread with reduced-oil salad dressing, piled with lettuce, salad and prawns.
2. Contents of small tin of baked beans, plus chopped salad of lettuce, tomatoes, onions, celery, cucumber.
3. 2 slices of bread with 1 oz (25 g) ham, 1 tomato and pickle.
4. 4 Ryvitas spread with 2 oz (50 g) pickle and 4 slices of turkey roll, or 3 oz (75 g) ordinary chicken or turkey breast plus 2 tomatoes. 1 piece of fruit.
5. Chicken leg (no skin) chopped salad (lettuce, tomatoes, onions, celery, cucumber), soy sauce or Worcestershire sauce plus natural yogurt.
6. 4 Ryvitas, low-fat cottage cheese, topped with prawns.
7. 4 Ryvitas, spread thinly with a low-fat soft cheese, plus salad.
8. 4 oz (100 g) red kidney beans, 4 oz (100 g) sweetcorn, plus chopped cucumber, tomatoes, onions tossed in mint sauce and natural yogurt.
9. 4 × 5 oz (4 × 150 g) low-fat, low-calorie yogurts – any flavour.
10. Salad of lettuce, tomato, cucumber, onion, grated carrot, etc., plus prawns, shrimps, cockles, lobster or crab (6 oz (175 g) total seafood) and Seafood Dressing (made by mixing 1 tablespoon of reduced oil dressing with 1 tablespoon tomato ketchup).
11. 4 Ryvitas, spread with any flavour low-fat cottage cheese, topped with tomatoes plus unlimited salad vegetables.
12. 1 slimmers' cup-a-soup. 2 Ryvitas with low-fat cottage cheese or soft cheese topped with salad vegetables. 5 oz (150 g) diet yogurt.
13. 1 cup of slimmers' cup-a-soup. 2 pieces fresh fruit. 5 oz (150 g) diet yogurt.
14. 1 cup of slimmers' cup-a-soup. 1 thin slice of bread, spread with a teaspoon of reduced-oil salad dressing and topped with salad and ¼ oz (6 g) grated low-fat cheddar.
15. Triple decker sandwich – with 3 slices light bread (e.g. Nimble) filled with 1 oz (25 g) turkey or chicken breast roll, or 2 oz (50 g) cottage cheese, lettuce, tomatoes, cucumber, slices Spanish onion. Spread bread with oil-free sweet pickle of your choice, e.g. Branston or similar, or mustard, ketchup, or reduced oil salad dressing.
16. 3 Ryvitas spread with 2 oz (50 g) pilchards in tomato sauce, topped with sliced tomato.

17. 2 slices wholemeal bread, spread with reduced-oil salad dressing made into sandwiches with 2 oz (50 g) tinned salmon and cucumber.
18. 4 slices wholemeal Nimble or similar light bread made into jumbo sandwiches. Spread bread with reduced-oil salad dressing and fill with lots of salad vegetables, e.g. lettuce, cucumber, onion, cress, tomatoes, beetroot, green and red peppers.
19. Rice salad: a bowl of chopped peppers, tomatoes, onions, peas, sweetcorn and cucumber mixed with cooked (boiled) brown rice and served with soy sauce.

Cold lunches
1. Seafood Salad (see page 52).
2. Chicken joint (with skin removed) or prawns, served with a chopped salad of lettuce, cucumber, radish, spring onions, peppers, tomatoes, with soy sauce or plain yogurt.
3. Vichysoisse (see page 37).
4. Chicken Liver Pâté (see page 34).
5. Smoked Haddock Terrine (see page 35).
6. Crab and asparagus open sandwiches: 2 slices wholemeal bread spread with Seafood Dressing. Spread fresh or tinned crab meat or seafood sticks on to the bread and decorate with asparagus spears.
7. Mixed Bean Salad (see page 88).
8. 4 oz (100 g) cottage cheese (any flavour) served with large assorted salad.
9. Large salad served with prawns, Tomato and Kiwi Salad (see page 86) dressed with low-fat natural yogurt.
10. 8 oz (225 g) carton low-fat cottage cheese, with two tinned pear halves, chopped apple and celery, served on a bed of lettuce and garnished with tomato and cucumber.
11. 3 oz (75 g) pilchards in tomato sauce, served with a large salad, and oil-free vinaigrette dressing.
12. 3 oz (75 g) salmon served with a large salad and yogurt flavoured with 1 teaspoon mint sauce.
13. 4 Ryvitas spread with low-calorie coleslaw, any flavour, and topped with salad.
14. Greek Island Salad (see page 31).
15. Jellied Chicken and Ham (see page 33).

Hot lunches
1. Jacket potato, topped with 8 oz (225 g) baked beans.
2. 2 slices wholemeal toast with 16 oz (450 g) tin of baked beans.
3. Jacket potato served with low-fat cottage cheese and salad (cottage cheese may be flavoured with chives, onion, pineapple, etc. but it must be 'low-fat').
4. Baked stuffed apples (one or two) filled with 1 oz (25 g) dried fruit, a few breadcrumbs and sweetened with honey or artificial sweetener, served with plain low-fat yogurt.
5. Watercress Soup (see page 39).
6. Lentil Soup (see page 36).
7. Minestrone Soup (see page 38).
8. Jacket potato with 1 oz (25 g) roast beef, pork or ham (with all fat removed) or 2 oz (50 g) chicken (no skin), served with Branston pickle and salad.
9. 2 slices wholemeal toast with small tin baked beans and small tin tomatoes.
10. Jacket potato served with sweetcorn and chopped salad.
11. Jacket potato served with grated carrot, chopped onion, tomatoes, sweetcorn and peppers, topped with natural yogurt.
12. Jacket potato filled with 4 oz (100 g) cottage cheese mixed with 4 teaspoons tomato puree and black pepper to taste.
13. Jacket Potato with Coleslaw (see page 86).
14. Jacket Potato with Chopped Chicken and Peppers mixed with yogurt.
15. Jacket Potato with Chopped Vegetables and yogurt dressing.
16. Jacket Potato with Prawns, Sweetcorn and 1 tablespoon reduced-oil dressing.
17. 2 oz (50 g) Dietburger (vegetarian), served with large salad.

PART 3: DINNERS
Select any one from each category: Starters, Main courses (vegetarian or non-vegetarian), Desserts

Starters
1. Crudités with Cocktail Dip (see page 32).
2. Tomato and Orange Soup (see page 39).
3. Orange and Grapefruit Cocktail. Remove all peel and pith from one

orange and a fresh ripe grapefruit and mix segments together (serves 2).
4. Marinated Haddock (see page 34).
5. Mussels in White Wine (see page 36).
6. Celery, Fruit and Yogurt Salad (see page 87).
7. Stuffed Courgettes (see page 32).
8. Tomatoes with Crab (see page 33).
9. Tomato and Pepper Soup (see page 37).
10. Mixed Vegetable Soup (see page 38).
11. Grapefruit segments in natural juice.
12. Melon balls in slimline ginger ale.
13. Clear soup.
14. Leeks Niçoise (see page 89).
15. Wedge of melon.
16. Half a grapefruit.
17. Braised Fennel (see page 89).

Main Courses
1. Chicken with Ratatouille (see page 74).
2. Hawaiian Haddock (see page 46).
3. Chicken Breasts with Mushrooms (see page 75).
4. Tandoori Chicken (see Recipe).
5. Fish Parcels with Cucumber (see page 44).
6. Fillet Steaks with Green Peppercorns (see page 62).
7. 8 oz (225 g) steamed, grilled or microwaved white fish (cod, plaice, whiting, haddock, lemon sole, halibut) served with unlimited boiled vegetables.
8. Spaghetti Bolognese (see page 58).
9. Marinated Chicken Kebabs (see page 73).
10. 3 oz (75 g) roast leg of pork with all fat removed, served with apple sauce and unlimited vegetables.
11. Barbecued Chicken (see page 74).
12. Mediterranean-style Cod (see page 42).
13. Gammon with Piquant Plum Sauce (see page 66).
14. Dijon-style Kidneys (see page 65).
15. Fillets of Plaice with Spinach (see page 48).
16. Normandy Chicken with Apples and Cider (see page 71).
17. Petits Poussins with Apples and Cranberries (see page 72).

18. Basque Rabbit (see page 82).
19. Glazed Duck Breasts with Cherry Sauce (see page 78).
20. Goulash (see page 60).
21. Turkey Escalopes with Grand Marnier (see page 77).
22. Rich Beef Casserole (see page 56).
23. Spicy Meat Balls (see page 57).
24. Roast Pork with Apricots (see page 67).
25. Chicken and Chicory Salad (see page 76).
26. Chilli con Carne (see page 58).
27. Provençal Beef Olives (see page 59).
28. Lamb's Liver with Orange (see page 65).
29. Turkey, Pineapple and Pasta Salad (see page 78).
30. Stuffed Marrow Rings (see page 61).
31. Guinea Fowl with Grapes (see page 80).
32. Minted Lamb Steaks (see page 64).
33. Beef Stroganoff (see page 60).
34. Braised Pigeons (see page 81).
35. French Lamb Hot-Pot (see page 64).
36. Rabbit with Prunes (see page 83).
37. Quarterpounder (100 g) Dietburger, served with unlimited vegetables or large wholemeal bap.
38. Steamed or grilled or microwaved trout, stuffed with prawns and served with a large salad or assorted vegetables.
39. 6 oz (175 g) calves' or lambs' liver, braised with onions, and served with unlimited vegetables.
40. Cod with Curried Vegetables (see page 42).
41. Trout with Pears and Ginger (see page 44).
42. Lemon Sole with Melon (see page 49).
43. Devilled Haddock (see page 46).
44. Lentil Roast (see page 92).
45. 6 oz (175 g) turkey (no skin) served with cranberry sauce, Dry-Roast Potatoes (see page 94) and unlimited vegetables.
46. 3 oz (75 g) roast lamb with all fat removed, served with Dry-Roast Parsnips (see page 94) and unlimited vegetables.
47. 6 oz (175 g) chicken (no skin) steamed, grilled, baked or microwaved, and served with unlimited vegetables.
48. Halibut with Herbs (see page 50).
49. Chicken and Leek Casserole (see page 70).

50. 3 oz (75 g) grilled or baked gammon steak or gammon rashers, with all fat removed, served with pineapple and unlimited vegetables.
51. Seafood Pilaff (see page 51).
52. 2 oz (50 g) bacon grilled, with all fat removed, served with grilled tomatoes, baked beans and jacket or boiled potatoes.
53. 4 oz (100 g) roast duck (all skin removed) served with unlimited vegetables.
54. Seafood Salad (see page 52).
55. Goujons of Sole with Orange and Kiwi (see page 47).
56. Grey Mullet with Tomatoes (see page 50).
57. Breton-style Squid (see page 53).
58. Skate with Leeks (see page 45).

Desserts

1. Meringue basket filled with raspberries and topped with raspberry yogurt.
2. Fruit Brulée (see page 100).
3. Stuffed apple served with plain yogurt.
4. 4 oz (100 g) fresh fruit salad mixed with 4 oz (100 g) natural yogurt.
5. Stewed fruit (cooked without sugar) served with 3 oz (75 g) diet yogurt.
6. Sliced banana topped with raspberry yogurt.
7. Fresh strawberries or raspberries served with diet yogurt.
8. Sliced banana topped with fresh raspberries or strawberries.
9. Fresh peaches sliced and served with fresh raspberries.
10. Two pieces of fruit of your choice.
11. 8 oz (225 g) fresh fruit salad.
12. Diet yogurt, including French-style set yogurt.
13. Stewed rhubarb sweetened with artificial sweetener, served with rhubarb diet yogurt.
14. Low-fat fromage frais, any flavour.
15. Spiced Plums (see page 101).
16. Prunes in Orange Pekoe Tea (see page 100).
17. Fruity Rum Compote (see page 101).
18. Honey Yogurt Fool (see page 102).
19. St Clement's Fool (see page 102).
20. Mango and Orange Mousse (see page 103).
21. Loganberry Mousse (see page 104).

22. Baked Apples with Apricots (see page 105).
23. Pears Aurora (see page 106).
24. Peach Ambrosia (see page 106).
25. Red Fruit Ring (see page 108).
26. Raspberry Fluff (see page 105).
27. Oaty Yogurt Dessert (see page 108).
28. Raspberry Yogurt Ice (see page 107).
29. Chestnut Meringues (see page 109).

Drinks

Tea and coffee may be drunk freely if drunk black, or may be drunk white so long as skimmed milk allowance is not exceeded. Use artificial sweetener whenever possible in place of sugar.

You may drink two alcoholic drinks per day. One drink means a single measure of spirit, a glass of wine, or small glass of sherry or half a pint (250 ml) of beer or lager. Slimline mixers should always be used and these and 'Diet' drinks may be drunk freely.

You may drink as much water as you like; sparkling mineral water tastes wonderful.

Grape, apple, unsweetened orange, grapefruit, pineapple and exotic fruit juices may be drunk in moderation.

Sauces and dressings

Sauces made without fat, and with low-fat skimmed milk from the daily allowance, may be eaten in moderation. Thin gravy made with gravy powder, but not granules, may also be served with main courses. Marmite or Bovril may be used freely to add flavour to cooking and on bread. For salads select any of the fat-free dressings (see recipes) and occasionally you can have the seafood dressing which has the closest taste to salad dressing, according to the menu selected. To make the seafood dressing mix together 2 tablespoons tomato ketchup, 1 tablespoon reduced oil salad dressing (e.g. Waistline, Heinz Weight Watchers) and a squeeze of lemon juice. Soy and Worcestershire sauce, lemon juice and vinegar may be eaten freely.

PART 4: DAILY NUTRITIONAL REQUIREMENTS

In selecting your menus, each day try to incorporate the following minimum quantities:

6 oz (175 g) protein food (fish, poultry, meat, cottage cheese, baked beans).
12 oz (350 g) vegetables (including salad).
12 oz (350 g) fresh fruit.
6 oz (175 g) carbohydrate (bread, cereals, potatoes, rice, pasta).
5 oz (150 g) low-fat yogurt.
10 oz (275 g) or 8 oz (225 g) semi-skimmed milk.

I would also suggest that one multivitamin tablet be taken daily to make doubly sure that you are getting all the vitamins you need.

PART 5: THE FORBIDDEN LIST

These foods are strictly forbidden whilst following the diet. Some will be reintroduced for the maintenance programme.

Butter, margarine, Flora, Gold, Outline, or any similar products.
Cream, soured cream, whole milk, Gold Top, Silver Top, etc.
Lard, oil (all kinds), dripping, suet, etc.
Milk puddings of any kind.
Fried foods of any kind.
Fat or skin from all meats, poultry, etc.
All cheese except low-fat cottage cheese unless otherwise stated in the
    diet menus.
Egg yolk (the whites may be eaten freely).
Fatty fish including mackerel, kippers, rollmop herrings, eels, herrings,
    sardines, bloater, sprats and whitebait.
All nuts except chestnuts.
Sunflower seeds.
Goose.
All fatty meats, including sausages, salami and pâté.
Pastry, cakes, biscuits, crispbreads (except Ryvita).
Chocolate, fudge, toffees, butterscotch.
Egg and cheese products, e.g. scotch eggs, quiche, etc.
Mayonnaise, French Dressing made with oil.

THE MAINTENANCE PROGRAMME

Losing weight is ironically always the easiest part of weight control partly because of the novelty value and partly because the instructions that we have to follow are quite clear. The problems arise once we *stop* dieting. Suddenly we feel free from the restrictions that have been placed upon us and it is all too easy to think, 'Great. I can now eat chocolate, chips and cakes!' In this respect the Hip and Thigh Diet is more helpful, because you cannot return to eating lots of the foods that made you fat in the first place — that is if you want to keep your new slimmer and trimmer figure. But you *can* relax a little and you *can* eat a wider variety of foods, including eggs, low-fat Cheddar cheese and fatless cakes.

On most diets the metabolic rate falls because the body adjusts to a reduced calorie intake and when people return to 'normal' eating the weight piles back on even though they are not overeating. It all seems so unfair doesn't it? Fortunately, because the Hip and Thigh Diet offers so much food — more calories than most diets would allow — the metabolic rate hardly falls at all. This is particularly evident with those who undertake regular exercise.

We lose weight when we consume fewer calories than our body needs, and we therefore make up the deficit from our stores of fat. After reaching our desired weight, we need to feed our body sufficient calories to maintain that new weight, but not ruin all our good work by eating too much and storing the remainder as fat again. It is a tricky situation, but so long as you keep a careful eye on the tape measure and the scales, you will soon become more confident in your ability to keep your weight constant. If you do over-indulge and you do gain weight, by returning to the diet for a few days you should be able to undo the damage quite quickly. But, if you wish to retain your slimmer hips and thighs, you must realize that a low-fat diet in the long term is essential. I don't think you need to worry too much with this point, however, as so many of my correspondents stated that their taste buds had been completely re-educated after following the diet — as were my own — and it was no effort at all to maintain their new figures. Many in fact completed questionnaires after they had been on the Maintenance Programme and they commented that with previous diets they had always regained the lost weight very quickly, but this time it was quite a different story. I could sense they were confident that they would never return to their bad, high-fat, eating habits ever again.

With all this in mind it is clear that this section is a very important one. It is vital to learn which foods may be eaten freely and which should be avoided so that we can have slim hips and thighs for ever!

You may prefer to release yourself from the restrictions of an actual diet. If so, please read carefully the following pages. They explain your nutritional requirements and which foods may be reintroduced into your daily diet, together with those which should still be avoided.

There is no need to tot up your daily intake of grams of fat. If you follow the basic principles already learned whilst on the diet, you really have nothing to fear. It is only when you start breaking the rules about forbidden foods on a regular basis that you will undo the good results that you have achieved. The very fact that we have avoided the need to count any form of units or calories throughout the diet has weaned us away from this negative habit. It would be a shame to start now with the counting of grams of fat. So relax and just remember what you've learned so far.

The following lists of foods and recommendations should form the pattern of foods consumed for a healthy diet. A daily diet made up of reasonable quantities from each category will ensure a balanced con- sumption of essential nutrients to maintain health and energy, without including unnecessary foods which add useless calories and lead to unwanted fat. A diet which follows these recommendations will encour- age a healthy digestion, and constipation problems will become a thing of the past.

Protein and minerals

A minimum of 6 oz (175 g) of meat, fish, eggs or cheese should be consumed daily.
½ pint (250 ml) skimmed or semi-skimmed milk should be consumed daily – maximum 1 pint (500 ml) per day.

Fish	Any type	Steamed, grilled or microwaved without fat
Meat	Any type, lean cuts only	Grilled, roast or microwaved, without fat, and with all fat trimmed off before cooking, or trimmed afterwards
Poultry	Any type	Grilled, roast or microwaved, without fat. Do not eat any skin or fat.
Offal	Any type	Steamed, baked or microwaved, without fat
Eggs		Cook in any way without the use of fat. Consume no more than 4 per week
Cheese	Preferably low fat e.g. Shape, Tendale, Edam	Restrict to 4 oz (100 g) per week if possible
Cheese	Cottage	Unlimited quantities may be consumed
Yogurt	Any type	Unlimited

right, Cocktail Dip (p. 32), Marinated Haddock (p. 34), Tomatoes with Crab (p. 33); overleaf, Minestrone (p. 38), Lentil Soup (p. 36), Watercress Soup (p. 39), Tomato and Pepper Soup (p. 37)

Vitamins
Approx. 12 oz (350 g) of fruit or vegetables should be consumed daily.

| Vegetables | Any type | Unlimited, but always without butter |
| Fruit | Any type | Unlimited. Serve on its own, or with Shape Single or top of the milk or ice cream |

Carbohydrates
A minimum of 4 oz (100 g) to be consumed daily.

Bread	Wholemeal or Crispbreads	Unlimited if eaten without fat; otherwise limit consumption to 3 slices of bread a day or 8 crispbreads
Cereal	Breakfast	1–2 oz (25–50 g) per day
Rice	Brown	2 oz (50 g) per day
Pasta	Fat free	Average portions 2–3 oz (50–75 g)
Potatoes	Boiled or baked	Unlimited if eaten without fat

Fats
Consume as little as possible.

| Low fat spread | Gold Outline Gold Lowest | Maximum of ½ oz (12 g) per day only. No butter or margarine |
| Cream | Single | 1–2 oz (25–50 g) very occasionally |

left, Melon and Prawn Surprise (p. 30), Jellied Chicken and Ham (p. 33), Stuffed Courgettes (p. 32); previous page, Smoked Haddock Terrine (p. 35), Mussels in White Wine (p. 36).

In addition, the following foods may be eaten in moderation
Milk puddings made with skimmed milk
Reduced-oil salad dressings, e.g. Waistline or Heinz Weight Watchers
Cakes made without fat
Ice cream
Pancakes made with skimmed milk
Yorkshire pudding made with skimmed milk in non-stick baking tin
Trifle made with only fatless sponge and custard made with skimmed milk, no cream
Cauliflower cheese made with low-fat cheese and skimmed milk
Sausages, if grilled well
Nuts – only very few and avoid Brazils, Barcelona nuts and almonds
Horlicks, Ovaltine or Drinking Chocolate
Sauces if possible made with skimmed milk, but *no* butter
Soups excepting cream soups
Soya, low-fat type

Avoid the following foods
Butter, margarine, Flora, or similar products
Oil, lard, dripping, etc.
Soya, full-fat type
Fried bread
Chapatis made with fat
Biscuits, all sweet varieties
Cakes, all except fat-free recipes
Milk, dried, whole
Cream, double, whipping, sterilized, canned
Cheese, all types except Edam, cottage, Tendale or Shape low-fat
    Cheddar
Cheese spread
Quiches, Scotch eggs, cheese soufflé, Welsh Rarebit, etc.
Fat from meat, streaky bacon
Skin from chicken, turkey, duck, goose, etc.
Salami, pâté, pork pie, meat pies, etc.
Sprats or whitebait, fried
Fish in oil
Anything fried, including mushrooms or onions
Desiccated coconut

Brazil nuts, almonds, Barcelona nuts
Chocolate, toffees, fudge, caramel, butterscotch
Mayonnaise
Marzipan
French dressing made with oil
Pastries
Pork scratchings
Avocados

HORS-d'OEUVRE
AND SOUPS

Many of these hors-d'oeuvre and soups make delicious light or warming lunchtime dishes. For instance the Tomatoes with Crab (page 33) are so easy to prepare, and can be served with a salad as a perfect light lunch. Then again, on a cold winter's day a bowl of lentil soup with a slice of wholemeal bread would make a warming and nutritious meal.

Alas, some of the recipes are rather substantial and are only suitable for Maintenance Dieters when served as the first course for dinner. These have been clearly marked and can still be eaten by Hip and Thigh Dieters as lunchtime meals.

HORS-d'OEUVRE

Melon and Prawn Surprise   30

Melon with Blackcurrant Liqueur (*Melon au Cassis*) 30

Chicory and Orange Salad   31

Greek Island Salad   31

Cocktail Dip   32

Stuffed Courgettes (baby marrows) (*Courgettes Farcies*)   32

Tomatoes with Crab   33

Jellied Chicken and Ham   33

Chicken Liver Pâté   34

Marinated Haddock   34

Smoked Haddock Terrine   35

Mussels in White Wine (*Moules à la Marinière*)   36

SOUPS

Lentil Soup   36

Vichysoisse   37

Tomato and Pepper Soup (*Potage Niçoise*)   37

Minestrone   38

Mixed Vegetable Soup   38

Tomato and Orange Soup   39

Watercress Soup   39

MELON AND PRAWN SURPRISE
SERVES 4–5

This dish can be prepared well in advance but it is best assembled only a short time before serving. You may find that a lot of juice comes from the melon balls and this will make the sauce too thin if all the ingredients are mixed together too early. Keep the melon well covered with cling-film while it is in the refrigerator, otherwise it will flavour other foods such as milk and bacon.

If you are serving individual melon halves, 225 g (8 oz) shelled prawns will be sufficient.

*2 Charantais, Ogen or small Rock melons or 1
    medium-sized Honeydew melon*
225–350 g (8–12 oz) cooked shelled prawns
8 whole cooked prawns
4 tablespoons low-fat fromage frais or yogurt
2–3 tablespoons tomato ketchup
A few drops Tabasco sauce
Salt
White pepper
A little paprika

1. If using Charantais, Ogen or Rock melons, cut them both in half. If using a Honeydew melon, cut a slice from the top. You may need to trim a little from the base of the melon (or each melon half) so that it stands firm, but take care not to cut too deeply into the flesh.
2. Scoop out the seeds from the melon.
3. With a melon baller, take out as many melon balls as possible. Scrape out the remainder of the flesh, taking care not to pierce the base of the melon. This surplus flesh can be used in a fruit salad.
4. If you wish, you can van-dyke the melon by cutting out small triangles from the cut edge with a small sharp knife or a pair of scissors, to create a serrated effect.
5. Mix the melon balls and shelled prawns together.
6. Take the whole prawns and, keeping the

heads attached, remove the shells from the tail part only. Cover and refrigerate the melon and prawns until required.
7. Mix the fromage frais or yogurt with the tomato ketchup. Season to taste with a few drops of Tabasco sauce, salt and white pepper.
8. To assemble the dish, first pour off any melon juice, then stir the melon and shelled prawns into the sauce. Check the seasoning.
9. Pile the mixture into the melon shells, garnish with the whole prawns and sprinkle a little paprika over the top.

MELON WITH BLACKCURRANT LIQUEUR
MELON AU CASSIS
SERVES 4

Cassis (blackcurrant liqueur) is easy to buy but as an alternative, mix 6 tablespoons blackcurrant cordial with 2 tablespoons brandy (or to taste) and use this instead.

2 Charantais, Ogen or Rock melons
6–8 tablespoons Cassis

1. Cut the melons in half and scoop out the seeds with a spoon. You may need to trim a little from the base of each melon half so that it sits firmly in a dish. Cover and refrigerate until served.
2. Just before serving, place each melon half in an individual dish. Fill the melon with the Cassis and serve.

CHICORY AND ORANGE SALAD
SERVES 4
for lunch; 6 as an hors-d'oeuvre

2 large heads chicory
2 oranges
350 g (12 oz) low-fat cottage cheese
15 g (½ oz) sultanas
1 teaspoon grated horseradish or horseradish
    relish
Salt
Freshly ground black pepper
A little paprika
1 bunch watercress

1. Separate the leaves of chicory, then wash
under cold running water and drain well. Do
not leave them to soak as this will make the
chicory bitter.
2. Grate the zest from one orange and
reserve. Using a small serrated knife, cut the
peel and pith from both oranges and then cut
out the segments from between the
membranes. Do this over a plate so that any
juice is kept. Squeeze the juice from the core.
3. Place the cheese in a bowl and stir in
sufficient orange juice to gain a creamy
consistency.
4. Roughly chop the sultanas and add them to
the cheese with the grated orange zest and
horseradish. Season with salt, freshly ground
black pepper and a pinch of paprika.
5. Fill the bottom half of each chicory leaf with
cheese mixture and arrange the leaves in
overlapping circles on a large round plate, using
the larger leaves on the outer rings and
decreasing in size as you get towards the
centre. Pile any surplus cheese in the centre.
6. Arrange the orange segments in the centre
of the plate, covering the cheese. Place a small
bunch of watercress in the centre of the orange
segments and surround them with a ring of
watercress sprigs or, if you prefer, arrange the
salad on individual plates.
7. Refrigerate until required and sprinkle a little
paprika over the oranges just before serving.

GREEK ISLAND SALAD
SERVES 4–6

1 small lettuce
½ cucumber
Salt
1 onion (preferably red-skinned)
1–2 large tomatoes
150 ml (5 fl oz) low-fat natural yogurt
2–3 tablespoons lemon juice
Salt
Freshly ground black pepper
1–2 tablespoons chopped fresh mint
A few black olives (Maintenance Dieters only)

1. Wash and drain the lettuce and remove any
tough or damaged leaves. Break the large
leaves into pieces; keep the small ones whole.
2. Dice the cucumber, sprinkle with a little salt
and leave to stand for 15–20 minutes. Then
wash under cold running water, drain and dry
well on kitchen paper.
3. Peel and slice the onion, and break the onion
slices into rings. Skin and slice the tomatoes.
4. To make the dressing, mix the yogurt with
the lemon juice, season with salt and freshly
ground black pepper, and add chopped mint to
taste. Refrigerate until required.
5. Mix the lettuce, cucumber, tomatoes and
onion together in a large salad bowl.
6. Just before serving, pour the dressing over
the top (or serve separately, if you wish). Mix
well. Maintenance Dieters can sprinkle the
olives, if used, over the top.

COCKTAIL DIP
SERVES 6–8
as a dip; 4–5 as an hors-d'oeuvre

This is an ideal pre-drinks dip. But if you prefer, arrange a selection of cut vegetables on individual plates around a small pot (such as a ramekin) filled with the dip, and serve it as an hors-d'oeuvre.

Because the amount of each vegetable will depend on how many different vegetables are served, I have given no individual quantities. (As a rough guide, 450 g (1 lb) of assorted vegetables will give the above servings.) Carrots, peppers, courgettes, celery, cucumber, cauliflower and small button mushrooms can all be used.

4–5 tablespoons low-fat fromage frais or yogurt
3–4 tablespoons tomato ketchup
A few drops Tabasco sauce
Salt
Freshly ground black pepper

1. Mix the fromage frais with sufficient tomato ketchup to colour and flavour. Season to taste with Tabasco sauce, salt and freshly ground black pepper. Spoon into a small serving dish.
2. Peel (if necessary), and wash a selection of vegetables. Cut carrots, peppers, courgettes, celery and cucumber into finger-length batons. Break the cauliflower into small florets, and cut the mushrooms into quarters.
3. Put all the vegetables (except the mushrooms) in cold salted water for at least half an hour, then drain well until dry.
4. Place the dish of dip in the middle of a large platter and surround with the vegetables in neat piles. Cover and refrigerate until served.

STUFFED COURGETTES
COURGETTES FARCIES
SERVES 4
Cooking time: 5 minutes

4 medium-sized courgettes (baby marrows)
1/2 small onion
2 tomatoes
225 g (8 oz) low-fat cottage cheese
75 g (3 oz) cooked shelled prawns
A few drops Tabasco sauce
Salt
Freshly ground black pepper

1. Trim both ends from the courgettes, removing as little flesh as possible. Cut each courgette in half lengthways. Place in a pan of boiling salted water and cook for about 5 minutes. Drain and place under cold running water until completely cold. Drain well again.
2. With a melon baller or a small teaspoon, scoop out some of the flesh, making a hollow down the length of the courgettes. Chop the scooped-out flesh and put in a sieve to drain.
3. Peel and grate or very finely chop the onion.
4. Skin (page 97) de-seed and chop the tomatoes.
5. Coarsely chop 50 g (2 oz) of the prawns.
6. Mix the tomatoes, onion, chopped prawns, chopped courgette and low-fat cottage cheese together. Season to taste with Tabasco, salt and freshly ground black pepper.
7. Pile the mixture into the courgette shells and garnish with the remaining prawns.
8. Refrigerate until served.

Hawaiian Haddock (p. 46), Devilled Haddock (p. 46)

TOMATOES WITH CRAB
SERVES 4

Tomatoes prepared in this way can also be served as a luncheon dish with salad.

4 medium-sized tomatoes
3–4 tablespoons low-fat fromage frais or yogurt
1–2 tablespoons tomato ketchup
A few drops Tabasco sauce
Salt
White pepper
225 g (8 oz) cooked white crabmeat
Fresh chopped parsley, to garnish
1 bunch watercress or a few lettuce leaves

1. Place each tomato stalk side down and, with a sharp knife, cut into six or seven segments almost down to the base, so that it opens out like a flower. With a teaspoon, scoop out the core and seeds.
2. Mix the low-fat fromage frais with the tomato ketchup and season with the Tabasco sauce, salt and white pepper.
3. Use a little of this sauce to moisten the crabmeat, then spoon the crabmeat into the tomato shells.
4. Sprinkle a little chopped parsley over each filled tomato and arrange them on a serving dish or individual plates. Garnish with the watercress or lettuce leaves.
5. Refrigerate until required.
6. Serve the rest of the sauce separately.

Grey Mullet with Tomatoes (p. 50), Breton-style Squid (p. 53)

JELLIED CHICKEN AND HAM
(Maintenance Diet hors-d'oeuvre or lunch; Hip and Thigh Diet lunch only)
SERVES 4

This dish can be used for a light luncheon or buffet if you make it in a ring mould or soufflé dish. You can double the quantities of meat but only 600 ml (1 pint) aspic will be needed.

100 g (4 oz) cooked chicken
100 g (4 oz) lean cooked ham
15 g (½ oz) aspic powder
300 ml (10 fl oz) boiling water
2–3 tablespoons dry sherry (optional)
1 tablespoon fresh chopped parsley
A few lettuce leaves, shredded (optional)
4 sprigs parsley

1. Remove all skin and fat from the chicken. Cut the ham and chicken into small dice, mix well, then divide between four ramekins or moulds.
2. If sherry is to be used, omit 2–3 tablespoons boiling water from the 300 ml (10 fl oz). Dissolve the aspic in the boiling water and leave until cool but still liquid. Add the sherry (if used) to the aspic. Stir in the chopped parsley and pour over the meat. Refrigerate until set.
3. The jellied moulds can be turned out or served in the pots. If you wish to turn them out, lightly moisten four small plates. Quickly dip each ramekin or mould into hot water and immediately turn out into the centre of each plate. Slide the mould into the centre if necessary.
4. Shredded lettuce can be arranged around the moulds if you wish. Then garnish the top of each mould or pot with a small sprig of parsley. Refrigerate until served.

CHICKEN LIVER PÂTÉ

(Maintenance Diet hors-d'oeuvre or lunch; Hip and Thigh Diet lunch)
SERVES 3–4
Cooking time: 10–15 minutes
Setting time: 3–4 hours

---

225 g (8 oz) chicken livers
1 small onion
1–2 cloves garlic or ½–1 teaspoon garlic paste
2 tablespoons red wine
2 tablespoons brandy
Salt
Freshly ground black pepper

1. Remove the sinews and any yellow-coloured flesh from the livers. (The yellow comes from the gall bladder and tastes bitter.) Wash the livers and dry well on kitchen paper.
2. Peel the onion and fresh garlic. Finely chop the onion and crush the garlic. Place in a pan with the red wine, cover and simmer gently until the onion is tender.
3. Dry-fry (page 116) the livers in a heavy non-stick frying pan, until they are cooked but still pink in the centre.
4. When the onions are tender, raise the heat and reduce the red wine to about 2 tablespoons.
5. Place the livers with the onion, garlic, red wine and brandy, in a food processor or liquidiser. Process or liquidise at top speed until smooth. Season to taste with salt and freshly ground black pepper.
6. Place the pâté in a small dish, smooth over the top, cover and refrigerate until firm.
7. Serve with 25 g (1 oz) hot toast per person and a mixed or green salad.

MARINATED HADDOCK

SERVES 4
Marinading time: 8 hours or overnight

---

350 g (12 oz) uncooked smoked haddock
1 medium onion
1–2 small carrots
1 teaspoon coriander seeds
2 bay leaves
2 lemons
Extra lemon juice if necessary
2 tablespoons white wine vinegar or cider vinegar
1 teaspoon caster sugar
A few lettuce leaves, to garnish
4 slices lemon (optional)
4 sprigs fresh parsley or chervil

1. Skin the haddock and remove any bones. Cut the fish into finger-sized 5 cm × 1 cm (2½ inch × ½ inch) strips and place in a shallow dish.
2. Peel the onion and carrots. Cut the onion into rings and the carrots into julienne (matchstick) strips. Spread the vegetables and coriander seeds over the fish, and tuck the bay leaves under it.
3. Grate the zest from one lemon and squeeze the juice from both. Measure the juice and, if necessary, make up to 120 ml (4 fl oz) with extra juice. Mix with the grated zest and vinegar, and pour over the fish. Sprinkle the caster sugar over the top. Cover and refrigerate for 8 hours or overnight.
4. To serve, arrange a few lettuce leaves on individual dishes. Remove the bay leaves and place some of the fish and vegetables in the centre of each dish. Pour over a little of the marinade. Garnish, if you wish, with a twist of lemon and a sprig of parsley or chervil. Refrigerate until served.

SMOKED HADDOCK TERRINE

(Maintenance Diet hors-d'oeuvre or lunch; Hip and Thigh Diet lunch)
SERVES 4–5
Soaking time: 1 hour
Cooking time: 5 minutes

---

450 g (1 lb) smoked haddock
150 ml (5 fl oz) skimmed milk
25 g (1 oz) aspic powder
100 ml (3½ fl oz) boiling water
2 tablespoons dry sherry
4 thin slices lemon
*100 g (4 oz) plain, low-fat quark or low-fat soft cheese (**M**, see p. 117)*
White pepper
A little lemon juice (optional)
A few lettuce leaves, shredded
A few sprigs fresh parsley, to garnish

1. Place four or five ramekins or small moulds in a refrigerator or deep freeze until they are well chilled.
2. Soak the smoked haddock in cold water for about 1 hour. Drain well and poach in the skimmed milk for about 5 minutes until tender. Take the fish from the pan, remove the skin and any bones, and leave to cool. Reserve the milk.
3. Meanwhile, dissolve half the aspic powder in the boiling water. Leave to cool and then add the sherry.
4. When the aspic is still runny but starting to set, coat the base and sides of each ramekin or mould. Place a thin slice of lemon in each one and when it has set, pour on a little more aspic. Return to the refrigerator.
5. Strain the milk in which the haddock was poached and measure out 85 ml (3 fl oz) into a pan. Bring the milk to the boil, remove from the heat and immediately add the remaining aspic powder. Stir until the powder has completely dissolved. Allow to cool slightly.
6. Flake the haddock with a fork and mix into the quark.

7. Stir in the aspic and milk mixture, and season to taste. It should not be necessary to add any salt but season with white pepper and, if you wish, a little lemon juice to give it a tang.
8. Spoon the mixture into the ramekins or moulds. Smooth over the tops and return to the refrigerator until set.
9. Lightly moisten four small plates. Quickly dip each ramekin or mould into hot water and immediately turn out into the centre of each plate. Slide the mould into the centre if necessary. Arrange a little shredded lettuce around each one and garnish the top with a small sprig of parsley. Refrigerate until served.

'Thanks a million. It works! It really, really works!' read the letter from Lorna Cowley, just one of many I received shortly after the publication of my *Hip and Thigh Diet* in January 1988. Lorna's letter continued, 'Prior to your book, which I ordered for 21 January, I was 38–34–42 (96–86–107 cm) and 11½ stone (73 kg) and quite despairing of ever being rid of an elephant rear and bulging tummy. By 31 January I could not stop admiring my new image in the long mirror! I was then 38–32–39½ (96–81–100 cm) and 11 stone (70 kg). My engagement ring I have been unable to wear for years; to my delight it fitted with ease last week!'

I knew my diet worked. It had worked for me and it had left me in no doubt as to its effectiveness when my original trial team put it to the test. The results really were staggering. I never once doubted my diet's effectiveness but I knew it was not easy to convince the media. *This* diet was different. *This* one worked. *This* one was easy to follow. *This* one made you feel good – not irritable like most diets. And, yes, it really *did* reduce the inches around those parts other diets didn't reach.

MUSSELS IN WHITE WINE
MOULES À LA MARINIÈRE
SERVES 4
Cooking time: 10–15 minutes

Dry cider can be used equally well in this recipe instead of white wine.

12 kg (4½ lb) mussels
1 small onion
1 clove garlic or ½ teaspoon garlic paste
(optional)
A few parsley stalks
1 sprig thyme
150 ml (5 fl oz) dry white wine
Freshly ground black pepper
1–2 tablespoons chopped fresh parsley

1. Wash the mussels well in several changes of water until they are free of sand and grit. Discard any which are broken or which remain open after being plunged into cold water or given a sharp tap.
2. With a small sharp knife, scrape the barnacles off the shells and remove the beards (the black threads hanging from the mussels).
3. Peel the onion and fresh garlic. Finely chop the onion, crush the garlic, and place in a large pan with the parsley stalks, thyme and dry white wine. Cover and simmer gently for about 5 minutes until the onion is nearly tender.
4. Add the mussels, season with freshly ground black pepper, cover and cook for a further 5–7 minutes over a good heat, shaking the pan occasionally, until all the mussels are open. If the odd mussel remains closed, discard it.
5. Pile the mussels into a large serving bowl or individual dishes. Pour over the cooking liquor, retaining the last few spoonfuls as these may contain grit. Sprinkle the mussels with chopped fresh parsley and serve immediately.

LENTIL SOUP
SERVES 6–8
Cooking time: 20–30 minutes

This soup is an ideal way to use up ham stock after boiling a piece of bacon. It freezes well and so you can, if you wish, freeze some for another time. After the bacon has been cooked allow it to become completely cold before using the stock for soup. Any fat will then have solidified on the top and can be removed. Leave any vegetables left in the stock – they will add extra flavour.

If you have insufficient stock, make up the quantity with water. The amount you start with does not matter too much. You can always adjust the consistency of the soup when it is made.

225 g (8 oz) orange lentils
1–2 carrots
2 onions
2 sticks celery
1 leek
1½–1¾ litres (2½–3 pints) ham stock
Freshly ground black pepper
Salt
Extra stock or water (if necessary)

1. Wash and drain the lentils. Peel the carrots and onions. Trim and wash the celery and leek. Thinly slice all the vegetables and add them, with the lentils, to the stock. Bring to the boil, cover and simmer gently for 20–30 minutes until the lentils and vegetables are tender.
2. Purée the soup in a food processor or liquidiser, or through a vegetable mill.
3. Return to the pan, and if necessary, add extra stock or water to thin the soup to the consistency that you like. However, do remember that it is meant to be a reasonably thick soup.
4. Check the seasoning and season to taste with freshly ground black pepper. It should only be necessary to add salt if water has been

added, as the stock is normally salty enough. Reheat and serve hot.

NB: This soup thickens if it is left until the next day, so if necessary, dilute it further with stock or water and check the seasoning again.

VICHYSOISSE

(Maintenance Diet dinner menu; or Hip and Thigh Diet lunch – no bread to be served, milk to be taken from allowance)
SERVES 6
Cooking time: 25–35 minutes

450 g (1 lb) leeks
175 g (6 oz) old potatoes
1 onion
450 ml (15 fl oz) chicken stock
Salt
White pepper
450 ml (15 fl oz) skimmed milk
3 tablespoons low-fat fromage frais or yogurt
Chopped fresh chives, to garnish

1. Trim the leeks, discarding the dark-green outer leaves. Wash well, drain and slice thinly.
2. Peel and slice the potatoes and onion. Place in a pan with the leeks and chicken stock. Season lightly with salt and white pepper, cover and simmer for 25–35 minutes until the vegetables are tender.
3. Remove from the heat and purée in a food processor, liquidiser or through a vegetable mill.
4. Add the skimmed milk and check the seasoning.
5. Either reheat or chill the soup before serving.
6. To serve, pour into hot or chilled soup bowls, and garnish each one with a spoonful of fromage frais and a few chopped fresh chives.

TOMATO AND PEPPER SOUP

POTAGE NIÇOISE
SERVES 4–6
Cooking time: 30–35 minutes

1 onion
2 cloves garlic or 1 teaspoon garlic paste
1 small green pepper
1 small red pepper
450 g (1 lb) ripe tomatoes or 1 × 400 g (14 oz) can tomatoes
100 g (4 oz) French beans
900 ml (1 ½ pints) chicken stock
Salt
Freshly ground black pepper
½ teaspoon caster sugar
1 tablespoon cornflour
Chopped fresh mixed herbs or dried Herbes de Provence, to garnish

1. Peel the onion and fresh garlic. Thinly slice the onion and crush the garlic.
2. Remove the stalk, core and seeds from the peppers and cut into small dice.
3. Skin the fresh tomatoes (page 97), de-seed fresh or canned tomatoes, and chop coarsely.
4. Top and tail the beans, and cut into 1 cm (½ inch) pieces.
5. Put all the vegetables in a pan and add the chicken stock and the juice from the canned tomatoes (if used). Season lightly with salt and freshly ground black pepper. Add the sugar and bring to the boil. Then lower the heat and simmer gently, uncovered, for 30 minutes.
6. When the vegetables are tender, mix the cornflour with a little water. Pour on some of the soup and mix well. Add the cornflour mixture to the pan and bring to the boil, stirring all the time. Boil for 2–3 minutes, then check the seasoning. Pour into a hot soup tureen and sprinkle a few herbs over just before serving. Serve hot.

MINESTRONE
SERVES 6–8
Cooking time:
Beans 1¾–2 hours plus soaking time
Soup 40–45 minutes

If using dried red kidney beans, they must be soaked in cold water for at least 5 hours or overnight. Then drain and rinse them well. Place in a pan and cover with water. Bring to the boil and BOIL RAPIDLY FOR 15 MINUTES. *This is essential.* Lower the heat and simmer gently for 1¾–2 hours until the beans just need a little more cooking. It is important that they are completely cooked before they are eaten. Do not add salt to the water as this will toughen them at this stage.

100 g (4 oz) dried red kidney beans or 1 × 400 g (14 oz) can red kidney beans
1 large onion
3 carrots
2–3 cloves garlic or 1–1½ teaspoons garlic paste
3 celery sticks
1 × 400 g (14 oz) can chopped tomatoes
1 litre (1¾ pints) beef or chicken stock
Salt
Freshly ground black pepper
100 g (4 oz) French beans or shelled peas
2–3 courgettes (baby marrows)
100 g (4 oz) cabbage
100 g (4 oz) egg-free spaghetti or cut macaroni
Chopped fresh basil or parsley, to garnish
A little Parmesan cheese (Maintenance Dieters only)

1. Prepare the dried beans, if used, as described in the introduction above. Drain well and place in a large saucepan. Canned beans should be drained but used later in the recipe (see Step 4).
2. Peel the onion, carrots and fresh garlic. Scrape and clean the celery. Chop the onion, celery and carrots, and crush the garlic. Add the vegetables to the pan with the tomatoes and stock. Season lightly with salt and freshly ground black pepper. Bring to the boil, cover and simmer for 30 minutes.
3. Meanwhile, top and tail the French beans, if used, and cut into 1 cm (½ inch) pieces. Trim and slice the courgettes. Shred the cabbage.
4. Break the spaghetti into short lengths. Then add the French beans or shelled peas, courgettes, cabbage, pasta and canned beans (if used) to the soup. Bring to the boil again, and cook for a further 8–10 minutes or until the vegetables and pasta are tender.
5. Check the seasoning and pour into a soup tureen. Sprinkle the chopped fresh basil or parsley over the top just before serving and serve hot.
6. Maintenance Dieters can sprinkle a little Parmesan cheese over their bowls of soup.

MIXED VEGETABLE SOUP
SERVES 8–10
Cooking time: 20–30 minutes

This soup is so easy to make that larger quantities than usual are given. It reheats well, and you can freeze any extra for another time if you wish.

225 g (8 oz) old but firm potatoes
225 g (8 oz) carrots
225 g (8 oz) onions
225 g (8 oz) leeks
3–4 sticks celery
2–2.5 litres (3½–4½ pints) chicken stock
Salt
Freshly ground black pepper
Chopped fresh parsley or chives, to garnish

1. Peel the potatoes, carrots and onions. Wash and trim the leeks and celery.
2. Grate the potatoes and carrots and finely slice the onions, leeks and celery. (A food processor or mixer with grating and slicing attachments is ideal for this.)

3. Place the vegetables in a large pan with 2 litres (3½ pints) stock. Season with salt and freshly ground black pepper. Bring to the boil, cover and simmer gently for 20–30 minutes until all the vegetables are tender. If you prefer a smooth soup, purée the vegetables in a food processor or liquidiser or through a vegetable mill.

4. Add more stock to thin the soup if necessary. Check the seasoning, reheat and pour into a hot soup tureen. Sprinkle the chopped fresh parsley or chives over the top before serving. Serve hot.

TOMATO AND ORANGE SOUP
SERVES 4

This is a very quick and easy soup to make. It has a delicious but subtle blend of flavours.

100 ml (3½ fl oz) orange juice
600 ml (1 pint) tomato juice
Juice of ½ lemon
Salt
White pepper
1 small orange
Fresh chopped chervil, basil, parsley or chives, to garnish

1. Mix the orange juice and tomato juice together. Add the lemon juice, salt and white pepper to taste. Cover and refrigerate.
2. With a potato peeler, cut the peel very thinly from the orange, making certain that there is no pith on it as this will be bitter. Cut into very thin strips. Blanch in boiling salted water for 3–4 minutes, drain and chill under cold running water. Drain well again.
3. Squeeze the juice from the orange and add to the soup.
4. Pour the soup into a chilled soup tureen or individual bowls. Sprinkle a few strips of orange peel and some chopped fresh herbs over the top. Serve chilled.

WATERCRESS SOUP
(Maintenance Diet dinner menu; Hip and Thigh Diet lunch – no bread to be served, milk to be taken from allowance)
SERVES 4–6
Cooking time: 30–40 minutes

This soup can be made in advance and stored in the freezer. If you wish to freeze it, prepare it to the end of Step 4 only. Then defrost and follow Step 5.

1 large bunch watercress
450 g (1 lb) old potatoes
1 large onion
600 ml (1 pint) chicken stock
Salt
White pepper
300 ml (10 fl oz) skimmed milk
2–3 tablespoons low-fat fromage frais or yogurt

1. Wash and drain the watercress. Reserve a few small sprigs for garnish. Coarsely chop the rest, including the stalks.
2. Peel and slice the potatoes and onion.
3. Place the potatoes, onion and watercress in a pan with the stock. Season lightly with salt and white pepper. Bring to the boil, cover and simmer gently for 20–30 minutes until tender.
4. Purée the soup in a food processor, liquidiser or through a vegetable mill.
5. Return to the pan, add the skimmed milk. If the soup is to be served hot, reheat then whisk in the fromage frais and reheat again without boiling. If the soup is to be served chilled, add the fromage frais just before serving. Check the seasoning before serving and garnish with sprigs of watercress.

FISH

A wide selection of different fish has been suggested in these recipes but if you prefer you can adapt them to the fish of your choice. For example, cod could be replaced by barramundi, flathead or whiting, plaice by bream, halibut by snapper, and skate by flounder. Whatever fish you choose you will find many new, different and tasty dishes which will encourage you to eat fish as often as possible.

Dieters may select any dish (except those marked Maintenance Dieters only) for lunch or dinner menus. If taken as a dinner menu, unlimited vegetables including potatoes or rice may be served. However, avoid rice or potatoes if served as a lunch menu. Choose some green vegetables or carrots instead. Because some of the recipes include rice, they have been clearly marked 'Hip and Thigh dinner only'. Maintenance Dieters can eat all the dishes for lunch or dinner.

Microwave tips have been given for all the recipes in case you want to adapt them for this style of cooking.

FISH

Mediterranean-style Cod (*Cabillaud à la Mistral*)   42

Cod with Curried Vegetables   42

Baked Cod with Sweet and Sour Sauce   43

Fish Parcels with Cucumber   44

Trout with Pears and Ginger   44

Skate with Leeks   45

Devilled Haddock   46

Hawaiian Haddock   46

Goujons of Sole with Orange and Kiwi (*Goujons de Sole aux Oranges et Kiwi*)   47

Fillets of Plaice with Spinach   48

Lemon Sole with Melon   49

Halibut with Herbs   50

Grey Mullet with Tomatoes (*Mulet à la Provençale*)   50

Seafood Pilaff   51

Seafood Salad   52

Breton-style Squid (*Calmar Armoricaine*)   53

MEDITERRANEAN-STYLE COD
CABILLAUD À LA MISTRAL
SERVES 4
Cooking time:
Sauce 20–25 minutes
Fish 25–30 minutes
Oven: 180°C, 350°F (Gas Mark 4)

500–700 g (1¼–1½ lb) cod fillet
450 g (1 lb) ripe tomatoes or 1 × 400 g (14 oz)
  can chopped tomatoes
1 onion
1–2 cloves of garlic or ½–1 teaspoon garlic paste
200 ml (7 fl oz) dry white wine or cider
175 g (6 oz) mushrooms
75 g (3 oz) lean back bacon
Salt
Freshly ground black pepper
2 tablespoons chopped fresh parsley
4–6 tablespoons white or brown breadcrumbs
1–2 teaspoons low-fat spread (Maintenance
  Dieters only)

1. Skin the cod or ask your fishmonger to do this for you. Remove any bones. Cut into large pieces and place in an ovenproof dish. Cover and refrigerate until required.
2. To make the sauce, skin the fresh tomatoes (page 97), and peel the onion and fresh garlic. Chop the fresh tomatoes coarsely and the onion very finely. Crush the garlic. Place the tomatoes, onion and garlic in a pan (including the juice from the canned tomatoes, if used). Add the dry white wine or cider. Bring to the boil and simmer for 20–25 minutes until the onions are tender and the sauce has thickened. If using tinned tomatoes, make certain that the sauce has reduced by half.
3. Meanwhile, wipe and slice the mushrooms. Remove the rind and any fat from the bacon and cut into strips.
4. Place the mushrooms and bacon on top of the fish. Season lightly with salt and freshly ground black pepper. Sprinkle the parsley over the top and pour on the sauce. Season lightly again.
5. Cover with a thick layer of white or brown breadcrumbs. Maintenance Dieters can dot a little low-fat spread over the top.
6. Bake, uncovered, in a preheated oven at 180°C, 350°F (Gas Mark 4) for 25–30 minutes until the fish is tender and the topping is crunchy. Serve hot.

Microwave
I prefer conventional cooking for this recipe as the top will not turn crunchy in a microwave. However, if you wish, the sauce and the completed dish can be cooked in the microwave and transferred to a conventional oven for the last 10–15 minutes to crisp the top.

Suggested Vegetables
Any green vegetable, carrots, jacket or boiled potatoes.

COD WITH CURRIED VEGETABLES
SERVES 4
Cooking time: 20–25 minutes

---

4 × 225 g (8 oz) cod cutlets or fillets
1 onion
1 small carrot
1–2 cloves garlic or ½–1 teaspoon garlic paste
1 stick celery
1 small leek
100 g (4 oz) tomatoes
150 ml (5 fl oz) water or vegetable stock
2–3 teaspoons curry powder
1–2 teaspoons juice from mango chutney
Salt
Freshly ground black pepper
1 tablespoon lemon juice
A little chopped fresh coriander, to garnish

1. Wash the fish and cut off any fin bones from the cutlets. Form the cutlets into a neat shape.

2. Peel the onion, carrot and fresh garlic. Trim and wash the celery and leek.
3. Finely chop the onion and crush the garlic. Cut the carrot and celery into very thin julienne (matchstick) strips and thinly slice the leek.
4. Skin (page 96), and chop the tomatoes.
5. Place the celery in a pan with the water or stock and boil for 3–4 minutes. Add the onion, carrot, leek, tomatoes and garlic and cook for a further 3–4 minutes.
6. Add the curry powder and the juice from the mango chutney. Season to taste with salt, freshly ground black pepper and lemon juice. If necessary, boil the sauce rapidly for a moment or two to thicken. Check the seasoning, adding more curry powder or lemon juice, if you wish.
7. Place each cutlet or fillet in the centre of a square of aluminium foil. Season lightly. Spoon the sauce equally over each one and fold up the foil so that the fish is completely enclosed. Seal well.
8. Place the parcels in a steamer with a tightly fitting lid and cook over a pan of gently boiling water for 20–25 minutes, until the fish is tender.
9. Undo the foil and carefully lift the fish on to individual plates. Sprinkle the chopped fresh coriander over the top just before serving. Serve hot.

Microwave

The vegetables and fish can be microwaved but reduce the amount of liquid to 3–4 tablespoons and use greaseproof paper instead of aluminium foil.

Suggested Vegetables

Brussels sprouts, Carrots in Yogurt (page 91), Orange Rice Pilaff (page 93) or new potatoes.

BAKED COD WITH SWEET AND SOUR SAUCE
SERVES 4
Cooking time: 20–25 minutes
Oven: 180°C, 350°F (Gas Mark 4)

1 quantity Sweet and Sour Sauce (page 113)
4 × 225 g (8 oz) cod cutlets or fillets
1 lemon
Salt
Freshly ground black pepper
1 tablespoon chopped fresh parsley

1. Prepare the onion for the Sweet and Sour Sauce (page 113).
2. Wash the fish and cut off any fin bones from the cutlets and form them into a neat shape.
3. Squeeze the lemon. Place the cod in an ovenproof dish with 4 tablespoons water. Pour the lemon juice over the fish. Season lightly with salt and freshly ground black pepper and bake in a preheated oven at 180°C, 350°F (Gas Mark 4) for 20–25 minutes until the fish is tender. Baste occasionally with the water and lemon juice.
4. Meanwhile, prepare the Sweet and Sour Sauce (page 113).
5. When the fish is cooked, arrange it on a hot serving dish, pour over a little of the Sweet and Sour Sauce and serve the rest separately. Sprinkle the chopped fresh parsley over the top just before serving. Serve hot.

Microwave

This dish is very suitable for microwaving.

Suggested Vegetables

Brussels sprouts, carrots, spinach or green beans, Dry-roast Potatoes (page 94) or creamed potatoes (made with skimmed milk or low-fat natural yogurt).

FISH PARCELS WITH CUCUMBER
SERVES 4
Cooking time: 20–30 minutes
Oven: 200°C, 400°F (Gas Mark 6)

4 × 225 g (8 oz) cod cutlets
½ cucumber
100 g (4 oz) white button mushrooms
1 small onion
1 carrot
1 clove garlic or ½ teaspoon garlic paste
Salt
Freshly ground black pepper
A little allspice
Juice of ½ lemon

1. Wash the cutlets and cut off any fin bones.
Form the cutlets into a neat shape.
2. Peel the cucumber, cut it in half lengthways,
scoop out the seeds with a teaspoon and cut
the flesh into small dice.
3. Wash, trim and thinly slice the mushrooms.
4. Peel the onion and carrot. Slice the onion
thinly and cut the carrot into julienne
(matchstick) strips.
5. Blanch the carrot and onion in a pan of
boiling salted water for 3–4 minutes. Drain.
Place under cold running water until completely
cold, then drain well again.
6. Peel and crush the fresh garlic. When the
vegetables are well drained, place in a bowl and
mix with the garlic, cucumber and mushrooms.
Season with salt and black pepper.
7. Place each cutlet in the centre of a square of
aluminium foil. Season with salt, freshly ground
black pepper and a pinch of allspice.
8. Divide the vegetables equally between the
four parcels. Pile them on top of each cutlet and
sprinkle a little lemon juice on each one. Fold up
the foil so that the fish and vegetables are
completely enclosed. Seal well.
9. Place on a baking tray and cook in a
preheated oven at 200°C, 400°F (Gas Mark 6)
for 20–30 minutes, or cook in a steamer over a
pan of boiling water for 20–25 minutes, until

the fish and vegetables are tender.
10. Arrange the parcels on a hot serving dish
and bring to the table unopened so that none
of the wonderful aroma escapes. Serve hot.

Microwave
This dish can be microwaved but use
greaseproof paper instead of aluminium foil.

Suggested Vegetables
Braised Fennel (p. 89), green beans, or peas,
Hip and Thigh Duchess Potatoes (p. 95).

TROUT WITH PEARS AND GINGER
SERVES 4
Cooking time: 40–45 minutes
Oven: 180°C, 350°F (Gas Mark 4)

4 × 225 g (8 oz) trout, gutted (approximate
   weight)
1 small onion
1 × 30 g (1 oz) piece root ginger
225 g (8 oz) ripe pears
50 g (2 oz) wholemeal breadcrumbs
1 teaspoon white wine vinegar
Salt
Freshly ground black pepper
3 tablespoons ginger wine (preferably green)
3 tablespoons orange juice
1 tablespoon chopped fresh parsley or chervil

1. With a sharp knife, scrape the scales from
each trout. Place underside-down on a board
and press firmly along the backbone.
2. Turn the fish over and run a finger and
thumb along each side of the backbone, freeing
the flesh from the bone. With a pair of scissors,
cut the backbone near the tail and near the
head. Discard the backbone and remove any
loose bones in the flesh.
3. Using the scissors again, cut the fins from the
fish and trim the tail.
4. Peel and grate the onion.
5. Peel and grate 1 teaspoon root ginger.

6. Peel, core and finely chop the pears.

7. Mix together the onion, ginger, pears, wholemeal breadcrumbs and white wine vinegar. Season with salt and black pepper.

8. Season the inside of each fish lightly. Divide the pear and ginger mixture equally between the four trout. Spread the stuffing inside each one and fold the fish so that the stuffing is completely enclosed.

9. Place the fish side by side in an ovenproof dish. Pour over the ginger wine and orange juice, cover with a lid or aluminium foil and bake in a preheated oven at 180°C, 350°F (Gas Mark 4) for about 40 minutes.

10. Place the fish on a hot serving dish and pour over any cooking juices. Sprinkle the parsley or chervil over the top just before serving. Serve hot.

Microwave
This dish is suitable for microwaving.

Suggested Vegetables
Broccoli with Tomatoes and Mushrooms (page 91), Mange-tout (page 90), Hip and Thigh Duchess Potatoes (page 95).

SKATE WITH LEEKS
SERVES 4
Cooking time: 25–30 minutes

In this recipe, flounder may be substituted for skate. You will need one large or two small fish.

450 g (1 lb) leeks
150 ml (5 fl oz) dry white wine or cider
2 × 600 g (1 1/4 lb) wings skate (approximate
    weight)
1 small onion
1 bay leaf
6 black peppercorns
2 tablespoons white wine vinegar or cider vinegar
Salt
2 tablespoons low-fat fromage frais or yogurt
Freshly ground black pepper
Chopped fresh parsley, to garnish

1. Trim, wash and drain the leeks. Finely slice the white and pale green parts only.

2. Place the leeks in a pan with the dry white wine or cider, and 150 ml (5 fl oz) water. Season lightly with salt. Cook gently for 20–25 minutes or until the leeks are tender and the liquid has almost evaporated. If necessary, add a little water to moisten the leeks while cooking.

3. Meanwhile, wash the fish, then trim any loose skin or sinew from the large bone along the top of the wings of skate. Peel and slice the onion. Place the fish in a large saucepan with the onion, bay leaf, peppercorns and vinegar. Cover with water and season lightly with salt. Bring to the boil, cover and simmer gently for 15–20 minutes (10 minutes for flounder) until the fish is tender.

4. When the fish is cooked, lift it from the pan with a slotted spoon and place it on a board. Remove any skin and cut off the thick cartilage-like pieces of bone at the top of each wing. Cut each wing in half, place on a hot dish, cover and keep hot.

5. If you wish you can purée the leeks in a food processor or liquidiser or through a vegetable mill. I purée them for just a moment or two in order to keep some of the texture.

6. Return to the pan and reheat, stirring gently.

7. Whisk the fromage frais into the leek mixture. Season to taste. Pour two-thirds of the leek sauce on to a hot serving dish. Arrange the pieces of skate on top and trail over the rest of the sauce. Sprinkle the chopped fresh parsley over the top before serving. Serve hot.

Microwave
The fish can be microwaved but cook the leeks and the sauce according to the recipe. I found the leeks puréed more easily when they were cooked the conventional way, and fromage frais curdles very easily in a microwave oven.

Suggested Vegetables
Spinach, Mange-tout (page 90) or peas, green beans, carrots, new or creamed potatoes (use skimmed milk or low-fat natural yogurt).

DEVILLED HADDOCK
(Maintenance Diet lunch or dinner; Hip and Thigh Diet dinner only)
SERVES 4
Cooking time: 30–35 minutes

---

750 g (1 1/2 lb) haddock fillet
1 small onion
100 g (4 oz) small button mushrooms
1 clove garlic or 1/2 teaspoon garlic paste
1 × 400 g (14 oz) can chopped tomatoes
2 tablespoons Worcestershire sauce
1 tablespoon soy sauce
1 tablespoon chopped fresh mixed herbs (parsley, thyme, chervil, etc) or 1 teaspoon dried mixed herbs
1 scant teaspoon curry powder
A few drops Tabasco sauce
Salt
1/2 small green or red pepper
100–175 g (4–6 oz) white or brown long-grain rice
75 g (3 oz) frozen peas
Chopped fresh mixed herbs or just parsley, to garnish

1. Skin the haddock or ask your fishmonger to do this for you. Remove any bones and cut the fish into 2.5 cm (1 inch) pieces.
2. Peel and finely chop or grate the onion. Wipe and trim the mushrooms and cut into quarters. Peel and crush the fresh garlic.
3. Mix the tomatoes (including their juice) with the onion, Worcestershire sauce, soy sauce, mixed fresh or dried herbs, garlic, curry powder and a few drops of Tabasco sauce in a frying pan. Season to taste with salt, cover and simmer for 20 minutes.
4. Add the fish and mushrooms to the pan. Cover with a lid and simmer for a further 10–12 minutes until the fish is tender.
5. Meanwhile, put the rice in a pan of boiling salted water and cook until tender. Remove the core, pith and seeds from the pepper and cut into small dice. Five minutes before the rice is

cooked, add the pepper and peas. Drain well and arrange in a ring around the edge of a hot serving dish. Cover and keep hot.
6. Check the seasoning of the fish mixture and add another drop or two of Tabasco sauce if necessary. Pour the mixture into the centre of the dish. Sprinkle a few chopped fresh herbs or parsley over the top just before serving. Serve hot.

Microwave
The sauce, fish and rice can be microwaved but the sauce must be cooked long enough to concentrate the flavour.

Suggested Vegetables
Carrots and green beans, or a green salad to follow.

HAWAIIAN HADDOCK
SERVES 4
Marinading time: 2 hours
Cooking time: 15–20 minutes

---

4 × 225 g (8 oz) haddock cutlets
1 × 225 g (8 oz) can pineapple rings in natural juice
1–2 teaspoons Chinese chilli sauce
1 tablespoon demerara or palm sugar
1 tablespoon lemon juice
1 tablespoon soy sauce
1/2 teaspoon French mustard
1 clove garlic or 1/2 teaspoon garlic paste
Salt
Freshly ground black pepper

1. Wash the cutlets and cut off any fin bones. Form then into neat shapes and place in a shallow dish (shallow enough to go under the grill).
2. Strain the juice from the pineapple and mix it with 1–2 teaspoons chilli sauce, the demerara sugar, lemon juice, soy sauce and French mustard. Peel and crush the fresh garlic. Add it

to the sauce. Season to taste with salt and freshly ground black pepper, adding more chilli sauce if required.

3. Pour over the fish, cover and refrigerate for about 2 hours, occasionally spooning over the marinade.

4. Uncover the dish and place under a pre-heated grill for 15–20 minutes or until the flesh comes away from the centre bone when tested with a fork. Keep hot.

5. Cut four pineapple slices in half. Sprinkle with a little extra demerara sugar and place under the hot grill until lightly caramelised.

6. Serve hot, garnished with the caramelised pineapple slices.

Microwave
This dish will look and taste better if grilled conventionally.

Suggested Vegetables
Italian Cauliflower (page 92), carrots and new potatoes.

Goujons of Sole with Orange and Kiwi
GOUJONS DE SOLE AUX ORANGES ET KIWI
SERVES 4
Marinading time: 1 hour
Cooking time: 8–10 minutes

Fillets of plaice can be used instead of sole, if you prefer.

750 g–1 kg (1½–2 lb) single fillets of sole
2 oranges
100 ml (3½ fl oz) dry white wine
100 ml (3½ fl oz) orange juice
Salt
White pepper
1–2 kiwi fruit
1 heaped teaspoon arrowroot
2–3 tablespoons low-fat fromage frais or low-fat soft cheese
Chopped fresh chervil or parsley, to garnish

1. Skin the fillets or ask your fishmonger to do this for you. Both dark and white skins must be removed and discarded. Cut each fillet diagonally into 1 cm (½ inch) strips.

2. With a potato peeler, cut the peel very thinly from one of the oranges, making certain that there is no pith on it as this will be bitter.

3. Using a small serrated knife, cut the peel and pith from both oranges and cut out the segments. Divide each segment into 2–3 pieces. Do this over a plate so that any juice is kept.

4. Place the fish in a glass or china dish. Add the dry white wine, orange juice and peel. Season lightly with salt and white pepper. Cover and leave to stand for about 1 hour.

5. Peel and slice the kiwi fruit, then cut each slice in half.

6. Transfer the fish, liquid and orange peel to a shallow pan and poach the fish very gently for 2–3 minutes until tender, then lift the fish out of the pan very carefully with a slotted spoon. Cover and keep hot.

7. Strain the fish liquor into a clean pan and bring to the boil. Mix the arrowroot with a little water, add to the pan and bring to the boil, stirring all the time. Stir in the orange segments and the fromage frais. Check the seasoning and reheat without boiling. Pour over the fish.

8. Garnish with the slices of kiwi fruit and sprinkle a little chopped fresh chervil or parsley over the top just before serving. Serve hot.

Microwave
Do not microwave. The cooking time is very short and the sauce should not be microwaved.

Suggested Vegetables
This dish has a delicate flavour so vegetable accompaniments should not be too strong-tasting. You could serve it with French or green beans, steamed broccoli or courgettes (page 96), Orange Rice Pilaff (page 93) or new potatoes.

Fillets of Plaice with Spinach
SERVES 4
Cooking time: 20–25 minutes
Oven: 180°C, 350°F (Gas Mark 4)

8 × 75–100 g (3–4 oz) single fillets plaice
225–275 g (8–10 oz) fresh spinach or
    100–180 g (4–6 oz) frozen leaf spinach
100 g (4 oz) plain, low-fat quark or low-fat
    cheese
1 egg white
Salt
White pepper
2–3 slices onion
5–6 black peppercorns
1 bay leaf
300 ml (10 fl oz) dry white wine or cider
2 tablespoons lemon juice
1 teaspoon arrowroot

1. Skin the fillets or ask your fishmonger to do this for you. Both dark and white skins must be removed and discarded.
2. Wash the fresh spinach well. Cook fresh or frozen spinach in boiling salted water for 4–5 minutes until just tender. Drain well, pressing out as much water as possible with a potato masher, so that the spinach is very dry. (This is very important.)
3. Purée the spinach in a food processor or liquidiser or chop very finely. Mix the spinach with 50 g (2 oz) quark. Whisk the egg white lightly and fold into the mixture. Season to taste with salt and white pepper.
4. Divide the spinach mixture equally between the eight fillets. Spread the mixture on the skin side of each fillet, roll up and secure with a cocktail stick.
5. Place the rolls of fish in an ovenproof dish. Arrange the onion slices and black peppercorns down the side and tuck the bay leaf in the centre. Pour over the dry white wine or cider and the lemon juice, and season lightly with salt and white pepper.
6. Cover and cook in a preheated oven at

180°C, 350°F (Gas Mark 4) for 20–25 minutes until the fish is tender.
7. When the fish rolls are cooked, carefully lift them out of the dish with a slotted spoon. Remove the cocktail sticks and arrange the fish rolls on a hot serving dish. Cover and keep hot.
8. Strain the cooking liquor into a small pan and boil rapidly until reduced by one-third. Mix the arrowroot with a little water and add to the pan. Bring to the boil, stirring all the time. Remove from the heat and whisk in the remainder of the quark a little at a time. Reheat without boiling. Check the seasoning and pour around the fish rolls. Serve immediately.

NB: If you want to keep this dish hot before serving, complete it to the end of Step 7. Then cover the fish with a lid or aluminium foil and keep hot in a warm oven. Reduce the cooking liquor but finish the sauce and pour it around the fish just before serving it.

Microwave
The fish can be microwaved but the sauce cannot so cook the sauce according to the recipe. Quark curdles very easily in a microwave oven.

Suggested Vegetables
Carrots, Broccoli with Tomatoes and Mushrooms (page 91), French Country-style Peas (page 90), new potatoes or Hip and Thigh Duchess Potatoes (page 95).

Goujons of Sole with Orange and Kiwi (p. 47), Fillets of Plaice with Spinach (p. 48), Lemon Sole with Melon (p. 49)

LEMON SOLE WITH MELON
SERVES 4
Cooking time: 12–15 minutes
Oven: 180°C, 350°F (Gas Mark 4)

Plaice fillets can equally well be used for this dish, but do not use the skins as they will make the sauce and fish bitter.

8 × 75–100 g (3–4 oz) single lemon sole fillets
    (approximate weight)
1 small onion
2–3 parsley stalks
1 bay leaf
Salt
White pepper
300 ml (10 fl oz) dry white wine
2 tablespoons lemon juice
1 small Honeydew melon
225 g (8 oz) firm tomatoes
1 teaspoon arrowroot
4 tablespoons low-fat fromage frais or yogurt

1. Skin the fillets or ask your fishmonger to do this for you. Both dark and white skins must be removed and reserved. Take out any bones and fold each fillet in half with the skin side inside. Place the fish in an ovenproof dish and tuck the skins in along the sides of the dish to add flavour to the sauce.
2. Peel and thinly slice the onion. Arrange around the fish, then add the parsley stalks and bay leaf. Season lightly with salt and white pepper. Pour on the dry white wine and lemon juice, cover with a lid or aluminium foil and cook in a preheated oven at 180°C, 350°F (Gas Mark 4) for 12–15 minutes.
3. Meanwhile, cut the melon in half and scoop out the seeds. With a melon baller, take out as many melon balls as possible. Any surplus flesh can be used in a fruit salad.
4. Skin (page 97), de-seed and cut the tomatoes into small dice.
5. When the fish is cooked, arrange it on a hot serving dish, cover and keep hot.
6. Strain the cooking liquor into a pan to remove the skins, onion and herbs. Boil rapidly until reduced by two-thirds. If you prefer a thicker sauce, mix the arrowroot with a little water, add to the pan and bring to the boil, stirring all the time. Strain the melon balls so that they are free of juice. Whisk in the fromage frais and stir in the melon balls and chopped tomatoes. Reheat without boiling. Check the seasoning and pour over the fish just before serving. Serve hot.

Microwave
The fish can be microwaved but cook the sauce according to the recipe. Fromage frais curdles very easily in a microwave oven.

Suggested Vegetables
Spinach, French beans, peas or Mange-tout (page 90), carrots, new potatoes or Hip and Thigh Duchess Potatoes (page 95).

Seafood Pilaff (p. 51), Trout with Pears and Ginger (p. 44)

HALIBUT WITH HERBS
SERVES 4
Cooking time: 20–30 minutes
Oven: 180°C, 350°F (Gas Mark 4)

Sorrel looks rather like spinach but has a slightly acidic flavour. Many supermarkets now sell packets of fresh sorrel and it is very easy to grow in the garden. If sorrel is not available, use spinach instead.

15 sorrel or spinach leaves
1 handful parsley sprigs
3 stems mint
1 lemon
750 g (1 1/2 lb) halibut steaks
Salt
Freshly ground black pepper
150 ml (5 fl oz) dry white wine or cider
1 teaspoon arrowroot
3 tablespoons low-fat fromage frais or yogurt

1. Wash the sorrel or spinach, parsley and mint. Strip the leaves from the stalks. Blanch in boiling salted water for 1 minute. Drain, rinse under cold running water until completely cold. Drain well again.
2. Squeeze the lemon.
3. Wash the halibut steaks, place in an ovenproof dish with a lid and season with salt and freshly ground black pepper. Pour over the dry white wine or cider, 65 ml (2 1/2 fl oz) water and lemon juice. Cover and cook in a preheated oven at 180°C, 350°F (Gas Mark 4) for 20–30 minutes until the fish is tender. Remove the fish from the dish with a slotted spoon, cover and keep hot.
4. Strain the cooking liquor into a small pan, bring to the boil and boil rapidly until reduced by half.
5. Purée the herbs and sorrel or spinach with the cooking liquor in a food processor or liquidiser. Return to the pan and bring to the boil. Mix the arrowroot with a little water and add to the pan. Bring to the boil, stirring all the time. Whisk in the fromage frais and check the seasoning. Reheat without boiling.
6. Pour over the fish and serve immediately.

Microwave
The fish can be microwaved but cook the sauce according to the recipe. Fromage frais curdles very easily in a microwave oven.

Suggested Vegetables
French Country-style Peas (page 90), green beans, carrots, new potatoes or Hip and Thigh Duchess Potatoes (page 95).

GREY MULLET WITH TOMATOES
MULET À LA PROVENÇALE
SERVES 3–4
Cooking time: 30–40 minutes

Ask your fishmonger to gut the fish for you. Other white fish such as cod, haddock, hake, flathead, flounder or sea bream can also be cooked in this way.

1 onion
2 cloves garlic or 1 teaspoon garlic paste
450 g (1 lb) ripe tomatoes or 1 × 400 g (14 oz) can chopped tomatoes
120 ml (4 fl oz) dry white wine or cider
Salt
Freshly ground black pepper
1 × 750 g (1 1/2 lb) grey mullet (approximate weight)
1 lemon, to garnish
1 tablespoon chopped fresh parsley

1. To make the sauce, peel the onion and fresh garlic. Chop the onion and crush the garlic.
2. Skin (page 97), de-seed and chop the fresh tomatoes. Drain the canned tomatoes (if used).
3. Place the onion, garlic, tomatoes and dry white wine or cider in a frying pan with a lid. Season lightly with salt and freshly ground black pepper, and simmer for about 10 minutes until the onion is tender.
4. Meanwhile, prepare the fish. With a sharp knife, scrape off the scales. Cut off and discard

the fins, head and tail. Cut the body into thick slices. Wash well under cold running water.

5. Place the fish in the tomato sauce and continue to simmer gently for about 20 minutes until tender. Transfer the fish to a hot dish.

6. Meanwhile cut the lemon into wedges.

7. When the fish is cooked, transfer it to a hot serving dish. Add the chopped fresh parsley to the sauce and check the seasoning.

8. Pour the sauce over the fish and garnish with the lemon wedges just before serving.

Microwave
This dish is suitable for microwaving.

Suggested Vegetables
Brussels sprouts, French beans or any green vegetable, new potatoes or Hip and Thigh Duchess potatoes (page 95) or rice.

SEAFOOD PILAFF
(Maintenance Diet lunch or dinner; Hip and Thigh Diet dinner only)
SERVES 4–6
Cooking time: 20–45 minutes (depending on type of rice used)

225 g (8 oz) smoked haddock fillet
1 small red pepper
1 medium onion
2 large tomatoes
100–175 g (4–6 oz) mixed long-grain and wild rice
450–600 ml (15 fl oz–1 pt) fish or vegetable stock
Salt
Freshly ground black pepper
450 g (1 lb) mussels (optional)
225 g (8 oz) scallops
100 g (4 oz) frozen peas
175 g (6 oz) cooked shelled prawns
1 lemon, to garnish
2–3 tablespoons lemon juice
A little paprika

1. Skin the smoked haddock and remove any bones. Cut into 2.5 cm (1 inch) pieces.

2. Remove the stalk, pith and seeds from the pepper, and cut into small dice.

3. Peel and chop the onion. Skin (page 97), de-seed and chop the tomatoes.

4. Wash the rice and place it in a large pan with the stock, pepper and onion. Season with salt and freshly ground black pepper. Bring to the boil, cover and cook until the rice is almost tender.

5. Meanwhile, prepare the mussels (page 36) if used. Wash the scallops and if they are large, cut into two or three pieces.

6. When the rice is almost cooked, add the smoked haddock, mussels and peas to the pan. Add a little more stock if necessary and cook for a further 5–8 minutes.

7. Once the rice is cooked and most of the liquid has been absorbed, add the scallops and prawns. Cook for 2–3 minutes only until the scallops are just cooked as they will toughen and shrink to very small pieces if overcooked.

8. Cut the lemon into wedges. Check the seasoning of the pilaff and stir in lemon juice.

9. Pile into a hot dish and sprinkle a little paprika over the top. Garnish with lemon wedges just before serving. Serve hot.

Microwave
This dish can be microwaved but I prefer to use conventional cooking as shellfish can be overcooked so easily.

Suggested Vegetables
Serve a green salad with, or after, this pilaff.

Any selection of fish and shellfish can be used in this recipe. If scallops are unavailable, use another 100–175 g (4–6 oz) prawns.

Look out for packets of wild rice mixed with long-grain rice. Wild rice is normally very expensive but the mixed packets now available in supermarkets are quite reasonable in price. The mixture gives a good contrast in textures and is excellent for this dish. However, you can, if you wish, use long-grain rice by itself.

SEAFOOD SALAD

(Maintenance Diet lunch or dinner; Hip and Thigh Diet dinner only)
SERVES 4–6
Cooking time: 15–20 minutes

This dish makes an excellent buffet party dish. If you prefer, you can use turmeric instead of saffron. It is less expensive and will give the same colour but not the same flavour. The feathery leaves of the herb fennel have an aniseed taste. If fresh herbs are not available, use ½ teaspoon fennel, dill or caraway seeds instead.

350 g (12 oz) haddock or other firm white fish
2–3 slices onion
1 bay leaf
Salt
White pepper
A pinch saffron or ¼ teaspoon turmeric
1 small bunch spring onions
100–175 g (4–6 oz) long-grain rice
75 g (3 oz) bean sprouts
1 small cucumber
450 g (1 lb) small tomatoes
2 tablespoons white wine vinegar or cider vinegar
4 tablespoons lemon juice
½ teaspoon French mustard
Sugar or artificial sweetener to taste
450 g (1 lb) cooked mussels (page 36)
8 whole cooked prawns
100–175 g (4–6 oz) cooked shelled prawns
2 teaspoons chopped fresh parsley
2 teaspoons chopped fresh fennel or dill
A little paprika

1. Wash the fish and place in a shallow pan with a lid. Add the onion slices and bay leaf. Season with salt and white pepper. Cover with water and poach gently for 15–20 minutes until the fish is tender. Using a slotted spoon, lift the fish carefully from the pan. Remove and discard the skin and any bones. Then flake the fish, keeping it in reasonably large pieces.

2. Place the saffron or turmeric in a cup and pour on 1 tablespoon boiling water. Leave to stand until required.
3. Wash the spring onions and cut into 5 cm (2 inch) lengths. Make several 2 cm (¾ inch) cuts down each end, to create a tassel effect. Leave in cold salted water for about 30 mins.
4. Wash the rice and cook in boiling salted water for 10–12 minutes or until tender. Rinse under cold running water and drain.
5. Blanch the bean sprouts in boiling salted water for 1 minute. Drain and place under cold running water until completely cold. Drain well.
6. Peel the cucumber, cut it in half lengthways, scoop out the seeds with a teaspoon and cut the flesh into 1 cm (½ inch) dice. Sprinkle a little salt over and leave to stand for 15–20 minutes. Then rinse under cold running water and drain.
7. Skin (page 97) and de-seed the tomatoes and cut into thin strips.
8. To make the dressing, whisk the vinegar, lemon juice and mustard together. Season to taste with salt, white pepper and a little sugar or sweetener.
9. Mix the saffron or turmeric with 1 tablespoon dressing. Stir into the rice.
10. Arrange the rice in a ring around the edge of a large serving plate.
11. Reserve six mussels in their shells to use as garnish. Remove the rest from the shells.
12. Take the whole prawns and, keeping the heads attached, remove the shells from the tail part only.
13. Mix the fish, shelled prawns, mussels, bean sprouts, cucumber and tomatoes in a large bowl. Pour on the remainder of the dressing and the chopped herbs. Pile into the centre of the dish and sprinkle a little paprika over the fish mixture.
14. Arrange the spring onion tassels around the dish between the rice and the fish mixture. Place four whole prawns in the centre and garnish each end of the dish with the remaining whole prawns and the mussels in their shells. Cover and refrigerate until served.

Microwave
The rice and fish except for the mussels can be microwaved separately.

Suggested Vegetables
Green salad and Tomato and Kiwi Salad (page 86).

BRETON-STYLE SQUID
CALMAR ARMORICAINE
(Maintenance Diet lunch or dinner; Hip and Thigh Diet dinner only – when served with rice)
SERVES 4
Cooking time: 40–50 minutes

This is an excellent recipe to use for *calmar* (squid). Because the fish is simmered gently, it is always tender. Small to medium-sized squid are best. This dish gets its name from Armorica, the ancient Roman name for Brittany.

1 kg (2 lb) squid
1 carrot
2 medium onions
1 clove garlic or ½ teaspoon garlic paste
1 sprig tarragon (optional)
3–4 tablespoons tomato purée
A good pinch cayenne pepper
A good pinch curry powder
300 ml (10 fl oz) dry white wine or cider
1 tablespoon brandy (optional)
Salt
Freshly ground black pepper
1–2 tablespoons low-fat fromage frais or yogurt

1. Prepare the squid (see right). Cut the tail into 1 cm (½ inch) rings and the fins and tentacles into two or three pieces.
2. Peel the carrot, onions and fresh garlic. Grate the carrot. Finely chop the onion and crush the garlic.
3. Place all the ingredients, except the fromage frais, in a pan. Season to taste with salt and freshly ground black pepper. Cover and simmer gently for 40–50 minutes until the squid and onions are tender. *Do not allow to boil*, as this will toughen the squid.

4. When the squid is tender, check the sauce. If it is a little thin, remove the squid with a slotted spoon, place it in a serving dish, cover and keep hot. Discard the tarragon (if used). Then boil the sauce to a coating consistency.
5. When the sauce has the correct consistency check the seasoning and, if necessary, add a little more cayenne pepper or curry powder – just sufficient to give a slight 'bite' to the sauce. Whisk in the fromage frais and reheat without boiling. Pour over the squid and serve hot.

Microwave
The squid will toughen immediately if overheated, so unless you can simmer it very gently in your microwave, cook it according to the recipe.

Suggested Vegetables
Serve with saffron-flavoured rice, and a green salad to follow.

TO PREPARE SQUID
1. Wash the squid. Pull the tentacles, head and innards away from the body section.
2. Cut the tentacles away from the head just above the eyes. Keep the tentacles but discard the head and innards.
3. Squeeze out and discard the small round piece of cartilage near the base of the tentacles.
4. Inside the tail, there is a long flat (quill-like) piece of cartilage. Pull this out and discard it too.
5. Pull the fins away from the body and reserve with the other edible parts.
6. Remove as much as possible of the pinkish-grey membrane from the tail, fins and tentacles. You can peel it away with your fingers from the tail and fins, and scrape the tentacles with a sharp knife.
7. Wash the squid well, running the cold water into the tail to remove the milky jelly inside. If you cut a small piece from the pointed end of the tail, it makes it easier to wash out the jelly. However you should only do this if the tail is to be cut into pieces, as in the recipe for Breton-style Squid. Sometimes the squid is stuffed and if so the tail should be left intact.

MEAT

'How can you cook meat without fat?' I have been asked this question so often. Well, in this chapter you will see how easy it is to cook old favourites and try out new ideas without using fat. Of course all meat contains some fat and, for this reason, you should limit each portion to 100 g (4 oz) lean trimmed meat. This will give about 75 g (3 oz) cooked meat.

All the recipes in this chapter are suitable for both Hip and Thigh Diet and Maintenance Dieters to eat as dinner menus, accompanied with a selection of vegetables. Potatoes and rice can also be served if you wish.

Microwave tips have been given for all the recipes in case you want to adapt them for this style of cooking.

Hip and Thigh Dieters are reminded that red meat should be restricted to two servings per week. Maintenance Dieters may eat it as desired.

MEAT

Rich Beef Casserole (*Boeuf en Daube*)   56

Spicy Meatballs   57

Spaghetti Bolognese   58

Chilli con Carne   58

Provençal Beef Olives (*Paupiettes de Boeuf Provençale*)   59

Goulash   60

Beef Stroganoff   60

Stuffed Marrow Rings   61

Fillet Steaks with Green Peppercorns (*Tournedos aux Poivres Verts*)   62

Moussaka   62

French Lamb Hot-pot (*Sauté d'Agneau à la Champvallon*)   64

Minted Lamb Steaks   64

Lamb's Liver with Orange (*Foie d'Agneau à l'Orange*)   65

Dijon-style Kidneys (*Rognons à la Dijonnaise*)   65

Gammon with Piquant Plum Sauce   66

Roast Pork with Apricots (*Roti de Porc aux Abricots*)   67

RICH BEEF CASSEROLE
BOEUF EN DAUBE
SERVES 4
Marinading time: 8–10 hours or overnight
Cooking time: 2–2¼ hours
Oven: 180°C, 350°F (Gas Mark 4)

This dish from the south of France gets its name from the earthenware pot in which it is traditionally cooked.

500 g (1¼ lb) lean stewing or braising steak
1 large onion
3 carrots
2–3 cloves garlic or 1–1½ teaspoons garlic paste
450 ml (15 fl oz) red wine
5–6 black peppercorns
3–4 juniper berries
1 bay leaf
75 g (3 oz) lean bacon or ham steak
2–3 tablespoons brandy (optional)
2 tablespoons tomato purée
Salt
Freshly ground black pepper
1–2 teaspoons arrowroot (optional)

1. Trim the steak, removing all fat. Cut into 2.5 cm (1 inch) cubes.
2. Peel the onion, carrots and fresh garlic. Slice the onion and carrots and chop the garlic.
3. Place the vegetables in a dish, lay the meat on top and pour over the red wine. Add the garlic, peppercorns, juniper berries and bay leaf. Cover and refrigerate for 8–10 hours or overnight. Turn the meat and vegetables in the marinade occasionally, if possible.
4. Place the meat, vegetables and marinade in a heatproof casserole. Cut the bacon or ham into thin strips and add to the casserole with the brandy, if used. Stir in the tomato purée and add more wine or some beef stock or water if necessary, so that the meat is completely covered. Season to taste with salt and freshly ground black pepper. Cover with a well-fitting lid and cook in a preheated oven at 180°C,

350°F (Gas Mark 4) for 2–2¼ hours until the meat is tender.
5. Remove and discard the peppercorns, juniper berries and bay leaf.
6. If you wish, the sauce can be thickened slightly. Using a slotted spoon, remove the meat from the sauce. Mix the arrowroot with a little water and add to the pan. Bring to the boil, stirring all the time. Return the meat to the pan, check the seasoning and serve, either in the cooking dish or poured into another hot one. Serve hot.

Microwave
This dish can be microwaved but reduce the wine to 300 ml (10 fl oz).

Suggested Vegetables
Carrots, Brussels sprouts or any other green vegetable, French or green beans, jacket or creamed potatoes (made with skimmed milk or low-fat natural yogurt).

right, Provençal Beef Olives (p. 59), Rich Beef Casserole (p. 56); overleaf, Spaghetti Bolognese (p. 58), Minted Lamb Steaks (p. 64) with Oven Chips (p. 94) and Carrots in Yogurt (p. 91)

SPICY MEATBALLS
SERVES 4
Cooking time: 30–40 minutes

225 g (8 oz) lamb's or pork liver
225 g (8 oz) lean minced beef
100 g (4 oz) wholemeal breadcrumbs
2 tablespoons tomato purée
1 teaspoon French mustard (preferably
    wholegrain)
Salt
Freshly ground black pepper
2 carrots
1 onion
1 × 400 g (14 oz) can chopped tomatoes
1 tablespoon demerara or palm sugar
1 tablespoon soy sauce
1 tablespoon white wine vinegar or cider vinegar
225–350 g (8–12 oz) egg-free tagliatelle or other
    egg-free pasta

1. Remove any membrane or veins from the liver. Process in a food processor with the minced beef until the mixture is smooth. Alternatively, chop the liver very finely and mix with the minced beef.
2. Mix the meat with the wholemeal breadcrumbs, tomato purée, and French mustard. Season with salt and freshly ground black pepper. Form into balls the size of a walnut and refrigerate until required.

3. To make the sauce, peel the carrots and onion. Grate the carrots and very finely chop or grate the onion. Place in a frying pan with a lid. Add the chopped tomatoes (including their juice), demerara sugar, soy sauce and vinegar. Season lightly, bring to the boil and simmer, uncovered, for 15 minutes.
4. Add the meatballs, cover and simmer for a further 15 minutes until the meatballs and vegetables are cooked. If the sauce is too thin continue cooking for another 5 minutes or so, uncovered. If it is too thick add a little water or beef stock until it has a coating consistency. Check the seasoning.
5. Meanwhile, put the pasta in a pan of boiling salted water and cook until just tender. Drain well. Arrange on a large serving dish and make a well in the centre.
6. Spoon the meatballs and sauce into the centre of the pasta. Serve hot.

Microwave
This dish can be microwaved but make sure the sauce reduces to a coating consistency.

Suggested Vegetables
Carrots, cauliflower, peas or beans.

Lynn Cook wrote: 'I now weigh 10 st 2 lbs (64.5 kg) and miraculously the weight has gone from all the right places. I have lost 2½ ins (6 cm) from my hips and 1½ ins (3.8 cm) from each thigh and 1 inch (2.5 cm) from my waist. When I have tried to diet in the past by counting calories, the weight was lost from the wrong areas and I didn't find the amount of food allowed satisfying enough. On your diet I am rarely hungry and find that I really enjoy the food.
I think this diet has revolutionized my eating habits and I will be able to follow the maintenance diet permanently (with the occasional lapse when eating out, which I don't need to feel guilty about).'

left, *Chilli con Carne (p. 58)*, *Spicy Meatballs (p. 57)*; previous page, *Gammon with Piquant Plum Sauce (p. 66)*, *Cucumber with Sage (p. 93)*, *Loganberry Mousse (p. 104)*

SPAGHETTI BOLOGNESE
SERVES 4
Cooking time: 35–40 minutes

This sauce can also be used for Stuffed Marrow Rings (page 61) so why not make an extra quantity and freeze it for another day?

450 g (1 lb) lean minced beef
1 onion
1 clove garlic or ½ teaspoon garlic paste
1 small green pepper
100 g (4 oz) mushrooms
1 × 400 g (14 oz) can tomatoes
150–300 ml (5–10 fl oz) beef stock
½–1 teaspoon dried basil or dried mixed herbs
Salt
Freshly ground black pepper
350 g (12 oz) long egg-free spaghetti
Chopped fresh parsley
A little Parmesan cheese (Maintenance Dieters only)

1. Dry-fry the mince (page 116) until it is lightly browned. Pour off any fat.
2. Peel the onion and fresh garlic. Chop the onion and crush the garlic.
3. Remove the stalk, pith and seeds from the pepper and cut into dice. Wipe, trim and slice the mushrooms.
4. Add the onion, garlic and diced pepper to the pan, together with the tomatoes (including their juice), a little of the beef stock and the dried basil or mixed herbs. Season to taste with salt and freshly ground black pepper. Simmer gently, uncovered, for about 20 minutes, then add the mushrooms and more stock if necessary to keep the meat moist. Continue cooking for another 15–20 minutes until the meat is tender.
5. Meanwhile, put the spaghetti in a large pan of boiling salted water and cook for 8–10 minutes until tender but still slightly firm.
6. Pile the spaghetti on to a large serving dish or individual dishes. Spoon the sauce into the centre, and sprinkle a little chopped fresh parsley over the top.
7. Maintenance dieters can sprinkle a little Parmesan cheese over as well.

Microwave
Dry-fry the mince (page 116). The spaghetti and the sauce can then be microwaved separately.

Suggested Vegetables
Serve a green salad with or after the dish.

CHILLI CON CARNE
SERVES 4
Cooking time: 50–60 minutes

1 onion
1 clove garlic or ½ teaspoon garlic paste
450 g (1 lb) lean minced beef
1 tablespoon chilli powder
1 × 400 g (14 oz) can chopped tomatoes
1 × 425 g (15 oz) can red kidney beans
1 tablespoon tomato purée
1 level teaspoon dried mixed herbs
300 ml (10 fl oz) beef stock
Cayenne pepper
Salt
100–175 g (4–6 oz) long-grain rice
1 green pepper
1 Spanish onion
1 teaspoon caster sugar
1–2 tablespoons red or white wine vinegar

1. Peel and finely chop the onion and fresh garlic.
2. Dry-fry the mince (page 116) until it is lightly browned. Pour off any fat.
3. Place the mince in a pan with the onion, chilli powder, canned tomatoes (including their juice) and the red kidney beans (drained). Stir in the tomato purée, dried mixed herbs and beef stock. Season to taste with cayenne and salt.
4. Simmer gently for 40–45 minutes until the meat is tender and most of the liquid has

evaporated. Check the seasoning, adding more cayenne pepper or chilli powder if you wish.
5. Meanwhile, put the rice in a pan of boiling salted water and cook until just tender. Remove the stalk, pith and seeds from the pepper and dice it. Peel the Spanish onion and cut into thin slices. Break into rings and place in a dish. Sprinkle the sugar and vinegar over the top and serve the onion and pepper separately as accompaniments.
6. If you wish, arrange the rice in a ring around the edge of a hot dish with the chilli in the centre, or serve the rice and chilli separately.

Microwave
Dry-fry the mince (page 116), then microwave on a low setting. Leave out the stock and add the beans for the last 3–4 minutes so they are just heated through.

Suggested Vegetables
Serve with a salad or any green vegetable.

PROVENÇAL BEEF OLIVES
PAUPIETTES DE BOEUF PROVENÇALE
SERVES 4
Cooking time: 1½–2 hours
Oven: 180°C, 350°F (Gas Mark 4)

---

4 × 75 g (3 oz) thin slices topside or skirt of beef
   (approximate weight)
100 g (4 oz) lean pork
2 tablespoons soft white or brown breadcrumbs
2 tablespoons chopped fresh parsley
½ teaspoon Herbes de Provence or mixed dried
   herbs
Salt
Freshly ground black pepper
100 g (4 oz) carrots (preferably slender ones)
100 g (4 oz) small onions
2 cloves garlic or 1 teaspoon garlic paste
300 ml (10 fl oz) tomato passata (page 97)
300 ml (10 fl oz) red wine or beef stock
A few black olives (Maintenance Dieters only)
Chopped fresh parsley, to garnish

1. Trim the slices of beef, removing all fat.
2. Mince the pork and mix it with the breadcrumbs, chopped fresh parsley and dried herbs. Season well with salt and freshly ground black pepper.
3. Divide the stuffing equally between the four slices of beef. Fold the edges of each slice over the stuffing, then roll up neatly so that the stuffing is completely enclosed. Secure the end with a cocktail stick.
4. Peel the carrots, onions and fresh garlic. Cut the carrots into 1 cm (½ inch) slices, quarter the onions and crush the garlic.
5. Dry-fry the paupiettes (page 116) over a good heat until they are sealed on all sides. Transfer to a heatproof casserole and add the carrots, onions and garlic.
6. Mix the tomato passata with the red wine or beef stock in the frying pan. Bring to the boil, taking care to mix in all the meat juices which may have caramelised in the pan. Season to taste and pour over the meat.
7. Cook in a preheated oven at 180°C, 350°F (Gas Mark 4) for 1½–2 hours until tender.
8. Transfer the paupiettes to a hot serving dish and remove the cocktail sticks. Keep hot. Maintenance Dieters can add the olives, if used, to the sauce. Check the seasoning and pour the sauce over the meat. Sprinkle chopped fresh parsley over the top just before serving. Serve hot.

Microwave
Dry-fry the meat (page 116), then microwave on a low setting. Reduce the amount of red wine (or beef stock) and tomato passata by one-third. If necessary, thicken the sauce with arrowroot.

Suggested Vegetables
French Country-style Peas (page 90) or any green vegetable, new or creamed potatoes (made with skimmed milk or low-fat natural yogurt).

GOULASH
SERVES 4
Cooking time: 2½–3 hours
Oven: 160°C, 325°F (Gas Mark 3)

It is possible to buy both a sweet and a hot
paprika. For a mild flavour use the sweet
paprika and for a spicy one use the hot paprika.
Or you could use some of each to give the
flavour of your choice.

450–500 g (1–1¼ lb) lean stewing beef
1 tablespoon plain white flour
350 g (12 oz) onions
1 × 400 g (14 oz) can tomatoes
450 ml (15 fl oz) beef stock
1 tablespoon tomato purée
1 tablespoon paprika
Salt
Freshly ground black pepper
½ teaspoon sugar
1 bay leaf

1. Trim the beef, removing all fat. Cut into
2.5 cm (1 inch) cubes and coat with the flour.
2. Peel and slice the onions.
3. Place the meat, tomatoes and onions in a
heatproof casserole. Pour on sufficient stock to
cover, and stir in the tomato purée and paprika.
Season with salt and freshly ground black
pepper, and add the sugar and bay leaf. Bring to
the boil.
4. Cover and cook in a preheated oven at
160°C, 325°F (Gas Mark 3) for 2½–3 hours
until the meat is tender. Add more stock if
necessary during the cooking time to keep the
meat moist.
5. Remove the bay leaf, check the seasoning
and serve hot.

Microwave
Microwave on a low setting. Reduce beef stock
to 300 ml (10 fl oz), adding more stock during
the cooking time if necessary.

Suggested Vegetables
Cabbage, Brussels sprouts, steamed
cauliflower, boiled rice or boiled potatoes.

BEEF STROGANOFF
SERVES 4
Cooking time: 20–25 minutes

1 large onion
1 clove garlic or ½ teaspoon garlic paste
175 g (6 oz) button mushrooms
200 ml (7 fl oz) red wine
1 tablespoon tomato purée
Salt
Freshly ground black pepper
450–500 g (1–1¼ lb) beef fillet steak
1 teaspoon arrowroot
2 tablespoons brandy (optional)
4 tablespoons natural low-fat yogurt or 3–4
    tablespoons low-fat fromage frais
Chopped fresh parsley, to garnish

1. Peel the onion and fresh garlic. Chop the
onion and crush the garlic.
2. Wipe, trim and slice the mushrooms.
3. Place the onion and garlic in a pan with the
red wine and tomato purée. Cover and simmer
gently for about 15 minutes until the onion is
tender. Add the mushrooms for the last 5
minutes. Season to taste with salt and freshly
ground black pepper.
4. Meanwhile, trim the meat, removing all fat.
Cut into 5 cm × 1 cm (2 inch × ½ inch) strips.
5. Dry-fry the meat (page 116) a little at a time
until brown on the outside but pink in the
centre.
6. When the onions are tender, mix the
arrowroot with a little water and add to the
pan. Bring to the boil, stirring all the time. Add
the brandy (if used). Boil for a moment or two,
then add the yogurt or fromage frais and the
meat. Reheat without boiling.
7. Check the seasoning and pour into a hot

dish. Sprinkle chopped fresh parsley over the top just before serving. Serve hot.

Microwave
Do not microwave.

Suggested Vegetables
Spinach, broccoli, carrots, white or brown rice.

STUFFED MARROW RINGS
SERVES 4
Cooking time:
Mince 20–30 minutes
Marrow rings 25–30 minutes
Oven: 200°C, 400°F (Gas Mark 6)

The meat sauce from Spaghetti Bolognese (page 58) can be used to fill the marrow rings instead of the filling given below. However, do make certain that most of the liquid in the sauce has boiled away. If you wish, you can make the mixture firmer by adding some breadcrumbs.

1 medium-sized marrow
350 g (12 oz) lean minced beef
1 medium onion
1 carrot
1/2–1 teaspoon dried mixed herbs
2 tablespoons tomato purée
300 ml (10 fl oz) beef stock
1 tablespoon Worcestershire sauce
Salt
Freshly ground black pepper
50–75 g (2–3 oz) fresh white or wholemeal
*   breadcrumbs*
A little Parmesan cheese (Maintenance Dieters
*   only)*
1 quantity Tomato Sauce (page 113)

1. Peel the marrow and cut into four thick rings. Scoop out the seeds. Place the marrow rings in boiling salted water for 2–3 minutes. Carefully lift them out of the pan with a slotted spoon, drain well and place on a non-stick baking sheet or roasting tin.
2. Meanwhile, dry-fry the mince (page 116) until it is lightly browned. Pour off any fat.
3. Peel the onion and carrot. Chop the onion and grate the carrot.
4. Add to the meat and cook for 2–3 minutes, then add the dried mixed herbs, tomato purée, beef stock and Worcestershire sauce. Season lightly with salt and freshly ground black pepper.
5. Bring to the boil and simmer gently, uncovered, for 20–30 minutes until the meat is tender. If necessary, add a little water or stock to keep the mince moist during the cooking time but do make certain that it has almost boiled away by the time the mince is cooked. The mixture needs to be moist but not runny.
6. When the mince is tender, add sufficient breadcrumbs to give a firm mixture. Check the seasoning.
7. Pile the mixture into the centre of the marrow rings. Maintenance Dieters can sprinkle a little Parmesan cheese over the top. Cover with greaseproof paper or aluminium foil and bake in a preheated oven at 200°C, 400°F (Gas Mark 6) for 25–30 minutes until the marrow is tender. Uncover for the last 8–10 minutes.
8. Meanwhile, make the Tomato Sauce (page 113).
9. Carefully remove the rings from the baking sheet with a non-scratch spatula or fish slice and place on a hot serving dish. Pour a little of the hot sauce over each one and serve the rest separately.

Microwave
Dry-fry the mince (page 116) and microwave but reduce the amount of stock to 150 ml (5 fl oz), adding more if necessary while the meat is cooking. The finished dish can also be microwaved.

Suggested Vegetables
Cabbage, Carrots in Yogurt (page 91), French Country-style Peas (page 90), Jacket or Hip and Thigh Duchess Potatoes (page 95).

FILLET STEAKS WITH GREEN PEPPERCORNS
TOURNEDOS AUX POIVRES VERTS
SERVES 4
Cooking time: 6–10 minutes

Rump or sirloin steak can be cooked by the same method.

4 × 100 g (4 oz) fillet steaks
1 tablespoon green peppercorns in brine
150 ml (5 fl oz) dry white wine
1–2 tablespoons brandy (optional)
3–4 tablespoons low-fat fromage frais or yogurt
Salt
Chopped fresh parsley
½ bunch watercress

1. Trim the steaks, removing all fat. Tie string around the outside of each fillet steak, or use a small meat skewer, to hold each one in a neat shape.
2. Drain and rinse the green peppercorns in cold water. Place in a pan with the dry white wine and boil rapidly until reduced by half.
3. Place the steaks on a wire rack in a grill pan and cook under a very hot preheated grill for 3–5 minutes on each side or until cooked the way you like them. Or you could cook them on a preheated grillade (page 116).
4. Reboil the sauce, adding the brandy (if used) and any meat juices which may have dropped into the grill pan (but no fat).
5. Remove from the heat and whisk in the fromage frais. Check the seasoning and add a little salt to taste. Reheat without boiling.
6. Remove the string or skewers from the steaks and place them on a hot serving dish. Pour over the sauce and sprinkle chopped fresh parsley over the top. Garnish with watercress and serve immediately.

Microwave
Do not microwave.

Suggested Vegetables
Braised Fennel or Celery (page 89), steamed broccoli or courgettes (page 96), Dry-roast Potatoes (page 94) or Hip and Thigh Duchess Potatoes (page 95).

MOUSSAKA
SERVES 4–6
Cooking time:
Aubergines 35–40 minutes
Moussaka 1¼–1½ hours
Oven: 190°C, 375°F (Gas Mark 5)

It is very difficult to give an exact weight for the aubergines. The skins must be large enough to line a 1–1.2 litre (1¾–2 pint) pudding basin or soufflé dish. I used three which weighed about 225 g (8 oz) each. However I only needed about three-quarters of the flesh. Mix any surplus flesh with 2–3 skinned (page 97), de-seeded and chopped tomatoes and 2–3 crushed cloves of garlic. Season to taste with salt and freshly ground black pepper, and place in a small dish. Cover and cook for about 30 minutes at the same time as the moussaka. Serve it with the moussaka or cold as an hors-d'oeuvre or with salad.

3–4 medium aubergines (see introduction above)
Salt
1 teaspoon oil
450–750 g (1–1½ lb) lean boneless leg or fillet of
*   lamb*
1 medium onion
2 cloves garlic or 1 teaspoon garlic paste
100 g (4 oz) mushrooms
2 tablespoons finely chopped fresh mixed herbs
*   (parsley, thyme, basil, chervil, etc) or*
*   ½ teaspoon dried mixed herbs*
A pinch cayenne pepper
Freshly ground black pepper
1–2 tablespoons tomato purée
4 egg whites
1 quantity Tomato Sauce (page 113)

1. Cut the aubergines in half. Remove the stalks and with a small sharp pointed knife cut the flesh all the way round about 0.5 cm (¼ inch) from the edge, taking care not to pierce the skin. Make deep diagonal cuts in both directions in the flesh. Sprinkle with salt, turn upside down and leave on a wire rack for 30 minutes. Rinse under cold running water and drain well.

2. Lightly brush a baking sheet or roasting tin with half the oil. Place the aubergines on this and add 2–3 tablespoons water. Cover with aluminium foil and cook in a preheated oven at 190°C, 375°F (Gas Mark 5) for 35–40 minutes, turning them once or twice, until they are tender.

3. Remove the aubergines from the oven and scrape the flesh from the skins, again taking care not to pierce them. Reserve the flesh. Brush the rest of the oil sparingly around the inside of a 1–1.2 litre (1¾–2 pint) pudding basin or soufflé dish. Line the dish with most of the aubergine skins, keeping some to cover the top.

4. Meanwhile, trim the meat, removing all fat. Cut into 2.5 cm (1 inch) cubes, then dry-fry (page 116) until browned on all sides. Cool slightly.

5. Peel the onion and fresh garlic. Grate or very finely chop the onion and crush the garlic. Wipe and chop the mushrooms.

6. Mince the meat in a mincer or food processor.

7. Mix the mushrooms, onion and garlic with about three-quarters of the aubergine flesh. Stir in the fresh or dried mixed herbs and cayenne pepper. Season to taste with salt and freshly ground black pepper.

8. Add the tomato purée to the meat, season to taste and mix well.

9. Whisk the egg whites in a clean dry bowl until they stand in stiff peaks. Then fold half into the meat and half into the aubergine mixture.

10. Place alternate layers of the aubergine mixture and the meat in the prepared mould. Fold the aubergine skins over to seal the top. Cover with greaseproof paper and stand the dish in a roasting tin almost filled with hot water. Return to the oven and cook for 1¼–1½ hours until the mould is firm to the touch.

11. Meanwhile, make the Tomato Sauce (page 113).

12. Heat the sauce. Turn the mould out on to a hot serving dish. Pour over a little of the sauce and serve the rest separately.

Microwave
The aubergines can be microwaved with a little water but cover well or the skins will dry out. Dry-fry the meat (page 116). The assembled moussaka can then be microwaved on a low setting.

Suggested Vegetables
Courgettes, French or green beans, salad, egg-free pasta or new potatoes.

This form of moussaka is made as a mould. The lamb is partly fried before it is minced, which keeps it beautifully moist. A very small amount of oil has been used in this recipe because I found it necessary to prevent the skins of the aubergines sticking to the baking sheet and the pudding basin.

Barbara Jones wrote: 'This diet has produced such a noticeable effect, especially on the hips/thighs, that everyone has commented on it. Lots of people have gone out and bought the book as a result. I feel fitter and healthier and, I have been told, look younger. I have lost weight in proportion and although I am still somewhat overweight (I want to lose another 7 lbs [3.2 kg]), I have gained a balanced figure, which makes me look slimmer. I have previously lost the same amount of weight, which I regained, but have never achieved my present shape.'

FRENCH LAMB HOT-POT
SAUTÉ D'AGNEAU À LA CHAMPVALLON
SERVES 4
Cooking time: 1–1 ¼ hours
Oven: 190°C, 375°F (Gas Mark 5)

450–500 g (1–1 ¼ lb) lean leg or fillet of lamb
1 medium-sized onion
350 g (12 oz) old, firm potatoes
1 tablespoon tomato purée
300 ml (10 fl oz) cider
Salt
Freshly ground black pepper
2 tablespoons chopped fresh parsley

1. Trim the meat, removing all fat. Cut into 2.5 cm (1 inch) cubes.
2. Peel the onion and potatoes. Finely chop the onion and thinly slice the potatoes.
3. Dry-fry the meat (page 116) until it is browned on all sides. Place in a heatproof casserole.
4. Mix the tomato purée and cider together in the frying pan. Bring to the boil, taking care to mix in all the meat juices which may have caramelised in the pan. Season to taste with salt and freshly ground black pepper.
5. Mix the onions, potatoes and chopped fresh parsley together. Season and pile on top of the meat. Pour the sauce over, cover with a lid and bake in a preheated oven at 190°C, 375°F (Gas Mark 5) for 1–1 ¼ hours until the meat and vegetables are tender. Uncover for the last 10 minutes of the cooking time to allow the potatoes to brown on the top. Serve hot.

Microwave
Dry-fry the meat (page 116), then microwave but reduce the amount of cider by one-third, and place in a hot oven for the last 10 minutes to brown the top.

Suggested Vegetables
Brussels sprouts, spinach or any other green vegetable.

MINTED LAMB STEAKS
SERVES 4
Cooking time: 10–15 minutes

4 × 100–150 g (4–5 oz) lamb steaks from leg of lamb, or chump chops
2 tablespoons redcurrant jelly
1 tablespoon chopped fresh mint
Salt
Freshly ground black pepper
A few sprigs fresh mint, to garnish

1. Trim the steaks or chops, removing all fat.
2. To make the glaze, heat the redcurrant jelly and 1 tablespoon water in a pan. Whisk until smooth and add the chopped fresh mint.
3. Brush the steaks or chops with the glaze, and grill under a preheated hot grill for 5–7 minutes on each side until they are cooked. Brush with extra glaze during the cooking time.
4. Brush the steaks again with the glaze and season with salt and freshly ground black pepper.
5. Arrange on a hot dish and garnish with the sprigs of fresh mint just before serving. Serve hot.

Microwave
Do not microwave. Grill according to recipe.

Suggested Vegetables
French Country-style Peas (page 90), Braised Fennel (page 89), Carrots with Yogurt (page 91), Oven Chips (page 94).

Barbecued Chicken (p. 74), Marinated Chicken Kebabs (p. 73)

LAMB'S LIVER WITH ORANGE
FOIE D'AGNEAU À L'ORANGE
SERVES 4
Soaking time: 30 minutes–2 hours
Cooking time: 10–15 minutes

350–450 g (12 oz–1 lb) lamb's liver
150 ml (5 fl oz) skimmed milk
1 orange, to garnish
Salt
Freshly ground black pepper
200 ml (7 fl oz) orange juice
¾ teaspoon arrowroot
¼ teaspoon chopped fresh or powdered thyme

1. Remove any membrane or veins from the liver. Place in a bowl, pour over the skimmed milk and leave to stand for 1–2 hours if possible but at least 30 minutes. This will help to keep the liver moist when it is cooked.
2. Wash and slice the orange. Cut each slice in half. Cover and put to one side.
3. Dry-fry (page 116) the liver until it is cooked but slightly pink in the centre, or cook under a preheated grill or on a preheated grillade (page 116). Season with salt and freshly ground black pepper when the liver is cooked.
4. Heat the orange juice in a pan. Mix the arrowroot with a little water. Add to the pan and bring to the boil, stirring all the time.
5. Arrange the liver on a hot dish and pour over the sauce. Sprinkle the fresh or dried thyme over the top and garnish, just before serving, with the orange slices. Serve hot.

Microwave
Do not microwave.

Suggested Vegetables
Carrots in Yogurt (page 91), Braised Fennel (page 89), Brussels sprouts or any green vegetable, potatoes of your choice.

Chicken and Leek Casserole (p. 70), Normandy Chicken with Apples and Cider (p. 71)

DIJON-STYLE KIDNEYS
ROGNONS À LA DIJONNAISE
SERVES 4
Cooking time: 10–15 minutes

10–12 lamb's kidneys
175 g (6 oz) mushrooms
200 ml (7 fl oz) red wine
4 tablespoons beef or lamb stock
1 heaped teaspoon arrowroot
75 g (3 oz) plain, low-fat quark or yogurt
1½ teaspoons Dijon mustard
Salt
Freshly ground black pepper
Chopped fresh parsley, to garnish

1. Skin the kidneys, cut them in half and remove the cores. Soak in cold salted water for 20 minutes. Drain well and dry on kitchen paper.
2. Wash, trim and slice the mushrooms. Season lightly, then cook gently in the red wine and stock for 7–8 minutes until tender.
3. Meanwhile, dry-fry (page 116) the kidneys until tender but still slightly pink in the centre. Place on a hot dish, cover and keep hot.
4. Mix the arrowroot with a little water, and add to the pan containing the mushrooms, red wine and stock. Bring to the boil, stirring all the time. Whisk in the quark and the mustard a little at a time. Reheat without boiling.
5. Check the seasoning and add more salt and freshly ground black pepper if necessary. Add the kidneys to the sauce. Pour into a hot dish and sprinkle chopped fresh parsley over the top just before serving. Serve hot.

Microwave
Do not microwave.

Suggested Vegetables
Braised Fennel (page 89), peas, beans, carrots, spinach, jacket, new or creamed potatoes (made with skimmed milk or low-fat natural yogurt), or egg-free noodles.

GAMMON WITH PIQUANT PLUM SAUCE
SERVES 6
Cooking time: 1 hour 20 minutes

Any lean cut of bacon or ham can be used for this recipe. I normally use a corner piece of gammon as this is about the right weight for me and it is not as expensive as the middle cut of gammon. It can be very lean but make sure there is not a thick layer of fat down one side. I also find the prime end of forehock a very lean and economical cut. If you wish, you can add more vegetables so that you can serve them with the meat. Parsnips can be included but don't use turnips as they give the stock a very strong flavour. Any leftover stock and vegetables can be used to make Lentil Soup (page 36).

1 × 1.5 kg (3 lb) gammon, ham or other bacon joint
2 carrots
2 onions
2–3 sticks celery
1–2 leeks (optional)
1 bay leaf
1 quantity Piquant Plum Sauce (page 112)

1. Tie the bacon with string so that it forms a neat shape. Soak smoked bacon in cold water overnight and green bacon for 2–4 hours.
2. Peel and wash the carrots, onions, celery and leeks (if used). Cut the onions into quarters and the carrots, celery and leeks into finger-length pieces.
3. Place the bacon joint in a large pan, cover with water, bring slowly to the boil and use a tablespoon to remove any scum which rises to the surface.
4. Add the vegetables and bay leaf and simmer gently, allowing 20 minutes for each 450 g (1 lb) of bacon and an additional 20 minutes.
5. Meanwhile, make the Piquant Plum Sauce (page 112).

6. When the bacon is cooked, remove it from the pan. Take off the string and peel away the skin and any fat. Slice the meat thinly and arrange on a hot serving dish. Pour over a little of the cooking liquor. If you are using the vegetables cooked with the meat, arrange them around the meat or serve them in a separate dish.
7. Serve some of the cooking liquor and the hot plum sauce separately.

Microwave
The gammon can be microwaved but cook the sauce according to the recipe.

Suggested Vegetables
French Country-style Peas (page 90), Broccoli with Tomatoes and Mushrooms (page 91), Braised Fennel or Celery (page 89), Dry-roast Potatoes (page 94) or Potato and Onion Bake (page 95).

Mrs Lynne Tindale wrote:

'After the birth of my second baby I seemed to be stuck at 11 stone (70 kg), but after following the Hip and Thigh Diet for eight weeks, I am back to the weight I was before I became pregnant, but now I find that even at my "normal" weight my hips, thighs and bottom are much slimmer than I can ever remember – jeans are quite baggy!

I also found that on the diet I even had enough energy to cope with a lively four-year-old boy and my new baby girl.'

ROAST PORK WITH APRICOTS
ROTI DE PORC AUX ABRICOTS
SERVES 4–6
Cooking time: About 2 hours
Oven: 200°C, 400°F (Gas Mark 6)

Canned apricots are used in this recipe for convenience but you could use 450 g (1 lb) fresh apricots or 175–200 g (6–7 oz) dried ones if you prefer. Cut the fresh apricots in half, remove the stones, place in a frying pan with a lid, and poach in the orange juice for 10–15 minutes. Cook them very gently so that they retain their shape. If using dried apricots, soak them overnight, then poach in the orange juice for 10–15 minutes. Whether using fresh or dried apricots, you may need to add a little more orange juice or water to thin the sauce. If you decide to use dried apricots, purée all the fruit and garnish with the watercress only.

1 × 1.5 kg (3 lb) joint from leg of pork
Salt
Freshly ground black pepper
1 × 400 g (14 oz) can unsweetened apricots (or see introduction above)
1 × 15 g (½ oz) piece root ginger
150 ml (5 fl oz) orange juice
A little caster sugar or artificial sweetener (optional)
1 small bunch watercress, to garnish

1. Rub the rind of the pork with a little salt, and season the meat with freshly ground black pepper. Place on a rack in a roasting tin and cook in a preheated oven at 200°C, 400°F (Gas Mark 6) for 30 minutes per 450 g (1 lb) and an additional 30 minutes.
2. Reserve six apricot halves for garnish. Purée the remainder (with the juice) in a food processor or liquidiser.
3. Peel and grate about 1 teaspoon root ginger. Add to the apricots and purée until smooth. Taste and add a little more ginger if necessary. Pour the purée into a pan and dilute to a pouring consistency with orange juice. Add a little caster sugar or sweetener if you wish.
4. When the meat is cooked, remove the rind and fat. Slice the meat thinly and arrange on a hot dish. Cover and keep hot.
5. Heat the sauce.
6. If the apricot halves are firm, slice them and place them, overlapping, at each end of the dish. Otherwise use them whole, cut side down. Pour over a little of the sauce.
7. Garnish with watercress just before serving and serve the rest of the sauce separately.

Microwave
Do not microwave unless you have a microwave/convector oven.

Suggested Vegetables
Italian Cauliflower (page 92), Broccoli with Tomatoes and Mushrooms (page 91), Cucumber with Sage (page 93), Dry-roast Potatoes (page 94) or Potato and Onion Bake (page 95).

Valerie Cousins wrote:

'Your Hip and Thigh Diet has completely changed my life. I am only a small person (5 ft 2 ins [1.57 m] in fact) and was not terribly overweight at 9 st 7 lbs (60 kg). I now weigh 8 st 9½ lbs (55 kg). I have been on your diet seven weeks, but am determined to stay on it further. I am told I look years younger and it's all thanks to you. I am so grateful to you . . . I seem to have so much confidence since regaining my teenage figure. Thanks. I am now able to put on my jeans; I feel like a teenager again. I have not stopped the diet as I wish to improve my figure further and you have given me the determination to do this. I have no intention of smothering my bread in inches of butter again – I have no wish to. This diet really has become a way of life for me.'

POULTRY AND GAME

Poultry and most game recipes are ideal for Hip and Thigh and Maintenance Dieters alike. You will find all sorts of interesting flavours in this chapter to add variety to your diet. Normandy Chicken with Apples and Cider (page 71) and Chicken Breasts with Mushrooms (page 75) are usually cooked with lashings of cream. These low-fat versions use yogurt or fromage frais instead. In other recipes, fruit, spices and vegetables add flavour without fat.

All these dishes can be served at dinner for all dieters except for Braised Pigeons (page 81). They are only suitable for Maintenance Dieters (or as a very special treat) because they have a higher fat content than other poultry or game.

Microwave tips have been given for all the recipes in case you want to adapt them for this style of cooking.

POULTRY AND GAME

Chicken and Leek Casserole   70

Normandy Chicken with Apples and Cider (*Poulet à la Normande*)   71

Petits Poussins with Apples and Cranberries (*Petits Poussins aux Pommes et Canneberges*)   72

Marinated Chicken Kebabs   73

Chicken with Ratatouille (*Poulet en Ratatouille*)   74

Barbecued Chicken   74

Chicken Breasts with Mushrooms (*Suprêmes de Poulet aux Champignons*)   75

Tandoori Chicken   76

Chicken and Chicory Salad   76

Turkey Escalopes with Grand Marnier (*Escalopes de Dinde au Grand Marnier*)   77

Turkey, Pineapple and Pasta Salad   78

Glazed Duck Breasts with Cherry Sauce   78

Guinea Fowl with Grapes (*Pintade à la Vigneronne*)   80

Braised Pigeons   81

Basque Rabbit (*Lapin à la Basquaise*)   82

Rabbit with Prunes (*Lapin aux Pruneaux*)   83

CHICKEN AND LEEK CASSEROLE
SERVES 4
Cooking time: 1–1¼ hours
Oven: 180°C, 350°F (Gas Mark 4)

4 chicken quarters or boned breasts
3–4 lean rashers back bacon
2 onions
2 carrots
1 clove garlic or ½ teaspoon garlic paste
4 small leeks
1 tablespoon plain white flour
1 × 400 g (14 oz) can chopped tomatoes
150 ml (5 fl oz) cider or chicken stock
½ teaspoon dried basil
½ teaspoon dried mixed herbs or Herbes de
    Provence
Salt
Freshly ground black pepper

1. Remove all skin and fat from the chicken.
2. Remove the rind and fat from the bacon and
cut into strips.
3. Peel the onions, carrots and fresh garlic. Slice
the onions and carrots and crush the garlic.
Wash and trim the leeks. If they are very long,
cut each one in half.
4. Dry-fry the bacon (page 116) in a heavy
non-stick frying pan or a cast-iron casserole.
Add the onions and cook for a moment or two,
stirring frequently. Stir in the flour and mix well.
Stir in the tomatoes (including their juice) and
the cider or stock. If using a casserole, add the
other ingredients. If using a frying pan up to this
point, you should now transfer the onion and
tomato mixture to a heatproof casserole. Place
the chicken pieces in the sauce, add the other
ingredients and season to taste with salt and
freshly ground black pepper.
5. Cover and cook in a preheated oven at
180°C, 350°F (Gas Mark 4) for 1–1¼ hours
until the chicken and vegetables are tender.
6. When the chicken is cooked, check the
sauce. If it is too thin, pour into a pan and boil
rapidly until reduced to a pouring consistency.

Check the seasoning and pour over the
chicken. Serve hot.

Microwave
Dry-fry the bacon (page 116) in a frying pan or
browning dish. Reduce the liquid by omitting
150 ml (5 fl oz) juice from the tomatoes. The
chicken and vegetables can then be
microwaved on a low setting. Reduce the
sauce, if necessary, according to the recipe.

Suggested Vegetables
Brussels sprouts, peas, beans or any green
vegetable, jacket, new or creamed potatoes
(made with skimmed milk or low-fat natural
yogurt).

Sharon Rice wrote:

'Before starting the diet I was slightly
overweight, yet despite working out
three times a week at the gym I was
unable to shift any weight from my hips or
buttocks; especially bad was the pad of fat
that had accumulated around the hips and
at the back of the hips. The gym instructor
said it was the hardest place to shift fat
from, but suggested some exercise which
I had to do hundreds of "repeats" of. I
perservered with the exercises until your
book came along, and hey presto! With a
combination of the diet and the exercises,
the flab started to disappear. Following
this routine I found the weight came off
steadily, and has stayed off.

The other good thing is that although
I'm no longer following the diet, I've found
my eating habits have changed for the
better. I don't miss butter in sandwiches –
it's no longer necessary – nor my
once-weekly portion of fish and chips –
far too fatty.

My hair and skin have improved no
end.'

NORMANDY CHICKEN WITH APPLES AND CIDER
POULET À LA NORMANDE
SERVES 4
Cooking time: 50–60 minutes
Oven: 180°C, 350°F (Gas Mark 4)

This dish is normally made with cream but I have used yogurt instead. If the sauce is too sharp for your liking, add a little sugar to taste.

8 chicken thighs or drumsticks, or 4 boned chicken breasts
2 medium-sized cooking apples
100 g (4 oz) button mushrooms
1 small onion
300 ml (10 fl oz) cider
2 tablespoons Calvados or brandy (optional)
Salt
White pepper
2–3 firm dessert apples
A little caster sugar
1 teaspoon arrowroot
150 ml (5 fl oz) low-fat natural yogurt
Chopped fresh parsley, to garnish

1. Remove all skin and fat from the chicken.
2. Peel, core and cut the cooking apples into large dice. Wipe, trim and cut the mushrooms into quarters.
3. Peel, grate or finely chop the onion.
4. Place the chicken in an ovenproof dish. Add the cooking apples, mushrooms, onion, cider and Calvados or brandy (if used). Bring to the boil and season to taste with salt and white pepper.
5. Cook in a preheated oven at 180°C, 350°F (Gas Mark 4) for 50–60 minutes until the chicken is tender. Allow extra time if necessary, according to the size of the chicken portions.
6. Using a slotted spoon, transfer the chicken and mushrooms to a deep hot dish. Cover and keep hot.
7. Meanwhile, peel and core the dessert apples. Cut into 1 cm (½ inch) thick slices and

sprinkle a little caster sugar over them. When the chicken is nearly ready, place the apple rings under a preheated hot grill until cooked and lightly caramelized.
8. Pour the cooking liquor into a pan and boil rapidly until reduced by half. Mix the arrowroot with a little water, add to the pan and bring to the boil, stirring all the time. Cook for a moment or two then add the yogurt and reheat without boiling. Check the seasoning, adding a little sugar if necessary, and pour over the chicken.
9. · Garnish the dish with the caramelized apple rings and sprinkle chopped fresh parsley over the top just before serving. Serve hot.

Microwave
Microwave the chicken on a low setting. Finish the sauce according to the recipe.

Suggested Vegetables
French Country-style Peas (page 90), carrots, spinach, egg-free pasta or jacket potatoes.

One reader, Linda Wood, wrote to me, saying:

'I am a lot more confident about myself because I know my weight will continue to come off, as I am eating so much more healthily. In fact, I don't feel as though I'm "rushed" on this diet; I feel this diet is a whole new way of eating for me. It certainly works for me, I feel tons better for it, and have lost all my guilty feelings about bingeing.
I want to say a big thank you.'

This diet does in fact prevent a lot of the feelings of hunger and deprivation which lead to bingeing. And if you can cure bingeing, you can be assured that you'll keep around your ideal weight for ever.

PETITS POUSSINS WITH APPLES AND CRANBERRIES
PETITS POUSSINS AUX POMMES ET CANNEBERGES
SERVES 4
Cooking time:
Poussins 30–40 minutes roasting time or
20–30 minutes grilling time
Apples 20–30 minutes
Oven: 200°C, 400°F (Gas Mark 6)

Petits poussins are small chickens weighing about 450 g (1 lb) each. They are available at most supermarkets and freezer centres but if you cannot find them, choose larger birds about 750 g–1 kg (1½–2 lb) and serve half a bird per person. If small cooking apples are not available, use a dessert apple such as Golden Delicious.

2 limes or lemons
4 petits poussins
Salt
Freshly ground black pepper
4 small cooking apples
2–3 tablespoons cranberry jelly
A few sprigs watercress or parsley, to garnish

1. Squeeze the juice from one of the limes or lemons. Cut the other into wedges and reserve.
2. Cut the poussins down the backbone with a pair of scissors. Flatten them well with one hand and push a thin skewer through the drumsticks (passing through the breast) to keep them flat. Sprinkle over most of the lime or lemon juice, season with salt and freshly ground black pepper, cover and refrigerate for 1–2 hours. If using larger birds, cut them in half by cutting through the breastbone as well.
3. Cut the apples in half (across not lengthways) and remove the cores, leaving just a little flesh at the base of each to prevent the jelly running through. Scoop the centres out slightly with a melon baller or teaspoon and

brush with lemon or lime juice. Fill the hollow apple halves with the cranberry jelly. Place on a non-stick baking sheet with 2–3 tablespoons water. Cover and bake in a preheated oven 200°C, 400°F (Gas Mark 6) for 20–30 minutes until tender but still holding their shape.
4. Meanwhile, cook the poussins under a preheated hot grill or in a preheated oven at 200°C, 400°F (Gas Mark 6). Grilled poussins take about 20–30 minutes. Roast poussins take about 30–40 minutes. Turn once or twice while grilling or roasting. To make certain that the chickens are cooked, prick the thighs with a fork. When the juices run clear the chicken is cooked.
5. Place a poussin (or half a larger bird) on each plate. Garnish with the apple halves and a few sprigs of watercress or parsley. Serve hot. (Hip and Thigh dieters should not eat the skin.)

Microwave
Can be microwaved but looks better when cooked according to the recipe.

Suggested Vegetables
Mange-tout (page 90), steamed broccoli or a green salad, jacket or Dry-roast Potatoes (page 94).

MARINATED CHICKEN KEBABS
SERVES 4–6
Marinading time: 2–3 hours
Cooking time: 15–20 minutes

Because oil is not used in this recipe, both the onions and mushrooms are precooked slightly to keep them moist.

2 lemons or limes
1 clove garlic or ½ teaspoon garlic paste
1 tablespoon clear honey
150 ml (5 fl oz) dry cider
Salt
Freshly ground black pepper
4 boned chicken breasts
100 g (4 oz) small pickling onions
100 g (4 oz) small button mushrooms
12 cherry tomatoes
2 courgettes (baby marrows)
1 small onion
100–175 g (4–6 oz) brown or white easy-cook
    rice
450–600 ml (15 fl oz–1 pt) chicken stock
25 g (1 oz) sultanas
25 g (1 oz) currants
1–2 tablespoons brandy or hot water
¼ teaspoon turmeric

1. Grate the zest and squeeze the juice from one of the lemons or limes. Cut the other into wedges and reserve. Peel and crush the fresh garlic.
2. To make the marinade, mix together the honey, dry cider, grated zest and juice of the lemon or lime and the crushed garlic. Season to taste with salt and freshly ground black pepper.
3. Remove the skin from the chicken and cut into 2.5 cm (1 inch) cubes. Place in a dish, pour over the marinade, cover and refrigerate for 2–3 hours. Turn the chicken occasionally in the marinade.
4. Meanwhile, carefully peel the pickling onions, leaving the root and stem ends intact so that the centres do not pop out while they are being precooked. Place in a pan of boiling salted water and cook for 5–8 minutes until almost tender. Take care not to overcook otherwise they will collapse. Drain well.
5. Trim and wipe the mushrooms. Place in a pan of boiling salted water and cook for 5 minutes. Drain well.
6. Wash and dry the cherry tomatoes and courgettes. Trim the courgettes, and cut into thick slices.
7. Drain the chicken, reserving the marinade. Then thread the cubes of chicken on to skewers, alternating with the courgettes, pickling onions, mushrooms and cherry tomatoes. Cover and refrigerate until required.
8. Peel and chop the onion, then place in a pan with the rice. Add the stock, season lightly, bring to the boil, cover and simmer gently until the rice is tender and all the liquid has evaporated.
9. Place the sultanas and currants in a cup with the brandy or hot water. Leave to stand.
10. Cook the kebabs under a preheated hot grill for about 15 minutes, basting occasionally with the marinade. Keep hot.
11. When the rice is cooked, drain the water (if used) from the sultanas and currants. If using brandy, stir it into the rice with the sultanas, currants and turmeric.
12. Pile the rice on to a hot serving dish and arrange the kebabs on top. Garnish with the lemon or lime wedges just before serving. If you wish to serve a sauce with the kebabs, use the one for Barbecued Chicken (page 74) or Tomato Sauce (page 113).

Microwave
The rice can be microwaved but cook the kebabs according to the recipe.

Suggested Vegetables
Serve this dish with a green salad.

CHICKEN WITH RATATOUILLE
POULET EN RATATOUILLE
SERVES 4
Cooking time: Ratatouille 20–30 minutes
Chicken 40–50 minutes
Oven: 190°C, 375°F (Gas Mark 5)

---

1 small aubergine
Salt
1 large onion
2 medium-sized courgettes (baby marrows)
1 small green pepper
2 cloves garlic or 1 teaspoon garlic paste
1 × 400 g (14 oz) can tomatoes
1 tablespoon chopped fresh basil or 1 teaspoon dried basil
Freshly ground black pepper
4 chicken breasts or chicken quarters
A little chopped fresh basil, to garnish

1. To make the ratatouille, cut the aubergines into 2.5 cm (1 inch) cubes, sprinkle 1 teaspoon salt over and leave on a wire rack for 20–30 minutes. Then place in a colander and rinse well under cold running water.
2. Peel the onion and trim the courgettes. Thickly slice the onion and courgettes. Remove the stalk, pith and seeds from the pepper and cut into strips. Peel and crush the fresh garlic.
3. Place all the vegetables, the tomatoes (including their juice), the fresh or dried basil and garlic in a pan. Season to taste with salt and freshly ground black pepper. Bring to the boil and simmer gently for 20–30 minutes, uncovered, until the vegetables are tender and most of the liquid has evaporated.
4. Remove and discard the skin from the chicken. Lay the pieces of chicken in an ovenproof dish and pour over the ratatouille. Cover and cook in a preheated oven at 190°C, 375°F (Gas Mark 5) for 40–50 minutes until the chicken is tender.
5. If chopped fresh basil is available, sprinkle a little over the top just before serving. Serve hot.

Microwave
Partly cook the ratatouille, add the chicken and finish microwaving on a low setting.

Suggested Vegetables
Serve with jacket potatoes or boiled rice, and any green vegetable or serve a salad after if you prefer.

BARBECUED CHICKEN
SERVES 4
Cooking time:
Sauce 30 minutes
Chicken 20–45 minutes

Any cut of chicken can be barbecued in this way. Drumsticks are ideal or you could use this as an alternative way of serving petits poussins (page 72). If you prefer, you can cook the chicken in a preheated oven at 200°C, 400°F (Gas Mark 6) for 35–40 minutes.

2 medium-sized onions
1 clove garlic or 1/2 teaspoon garlic paste
1 × 400 g (14 oz) can tomatoes
2 tablespoons Worcestershire sauce
1 tablespoon honey
1 teaspoon paprika (page 60)
Salt
Freshly ground black pepper
4 chicken quarters or 8 drumsticks
Half bunch watercress or parsley, to garnish

1. To make the sauce, peel the onions and fresh garlic. Finely chop the onions and crush the garlic. Place in a pan with the tomatoes (including their juice), Worcestershire sauce, honey and paprika. Season to taste with salt and freshly ground black pepper. Bring to the boil and simmer, uncovered, for 30 minutes until the onions are tender and the sauce has thickened slightly.
2. Remove all skin and fat from the chicken.

Brush well with the sauce and grill under a preheated hot grill for 25–30 minutes. The cooking time will depend on the thickness of the meat – chicken quarters will take longer than drumsticks. Turn once or twice while cooking, brushing them with more sauce. To make certain the chicken is cooked, prick the chicken with a fork. When the juices run clear, it is cooked.

3. Garnish with watercress or parsley just before serving and serve hot, with the remaining sauce served separately.

Microwave
Do not microwave.

Suggested Vegetables
Green salad and jacket potatoes.

CHICKEN BREASTS WITH MUSHROOMS
SUPRÊMES DE POULET AUX CHAMPIGNONS
SERVES 4
Cooking time: 50–60 minutes
Oven: 190°C, 375°F (Gas Mark 5)

4 boned chicken breasts
100 g (4 oz) lean bacon steak
1 onion
1 clove garlic or 1/2 teaspoon garlic paste
175 g (6 oz) button mushrooms
150 ml (5 fl oz) chicken stock
150 ml (5 fl oz) dry cider
2 teaspoons paprika (page 60)
Salt
White pepper
1 heaped teaspoon arrowroot
150 ml (5 fl oz) natural low-fat yogurt or 4 tablespoons low-fat fromage frais
1 tablespoon chopped fresh parsley or tarragon

1. Skin the chicken, dice the bacon and place them in an ovenproof dish.

2. Peel the onion and fresh garlic. Finely chop the onion and crush the garlic.
3. Wipe, trim and cut the mushrooms into quarters.
4. Add the onions and garlic to the chicken. Heat the stock and cider together, stir in the paprika, pour over the chicken and season lightly with salt and white pepper. Cook in a preheated oven at 190°C, 375°F (Gas Mark 5) for 50–60 minutes until the chicken is tender. Add the mushrooms for the last 10–15 minutes of cooking time.
5. Using a slotted spoon, transfer the chicken, bacon and mushrooms to a hot serving dish. Cover and keep hot.
6. Pour the cooking liquor into a pan and boil rapidly to reduce by half. Mix the arrowroot with a little water and add to the pan. Bring to the boil, stirring all the time. Cook for a moment or two, then add the yogurt or fromage frais, and chopped fresh parsley or tarragon. Reheat without boiling. Check the seasoning and pour over the chicken. Serve hot.

Microwave
The chicken can be microwaved on a low setting but finish the sauce according to the recipe.

Suggested Vegetables
Spinach, courgettes, Brussels sprouts or green beans, new potatoes or Hip and Thigh Duchess Potatoes (page 95).

TANDOORI CHICKEN
SERVES 4
Marinading time: 4–6 hours or overnight
Cooking time: 50–60 minutes
Oven: 190°C, 375°F (Gas Mark 5), then 160°C, 325°F (Gas Mark 3)

---

4 chicken quarters
2 cloves garlic or 1 teaspoon garlic paste
1 × 40–50 g (1 1/2–2 oz) piece root ginger
1 green chilli
1/4 teaspoon mustard powder
1 teaspoon coriander seeds
2 teaspoons garam marsala
1 teaspoon turmeric
1 tablespoon tomato purée
150 ml (5 fl oz) low-fat natural yogurt
Salt
Freshly ground black pepper
Red colouring (optional)
1–2 limes or lemons
Indian pickle, to serve

1. Peel the garlic and ginger and chop roughly.
2. Cut the chilli in half and remove the seeds. Take care not to touch lips or eyes with the fingers, as the juice of the chilli will make them sting. Wash hands immediately to remove any juices.
3. Place the garlic, mustard powder, coriander seeds, ginger, chilli, garam marsala, turmeric, tomato purée and yogurt in a food processor or liquidiser. Purée until smooth and season with salt and freshly ground black pepper. Add a little red colouring, if you wish.
4. Remove the skin and any fat from the chicken quarters. Prick them all over with a fork. Place in a large dish and cover with the marinade. Cover and refrigerate for 4–6 hours or overnight. Turn them in the marinade occasionally, if possible.
5. To cook, place the chicken quarters on a wire rack in a roasting tin and bake in a preheated oven at 190°C, 375°F (Gas Mark 5) for 30 minutes. Then reduce the temperature

to 160°C, 325°F (Gas Mark 3) for a further 20–25 minutes until the chicken is tender.
6. Meanwhile, cut the limes or lemons into wedges and reserve.
7. Garnish with the lime or lemon wedges just before serving. Serve hot, with Indian pickle.

Microwave
Do not microwave.

Suggested Vegetables
Green salad and boiled rice or the rice pilaff from Marinated Chicken Kebabs (page 73).

CHICKEN AND CHICORY SALAD
SERVES 6

This is an ideal buffet party dish or, if you prefer, you could use a half quantity as a light luncheon. It is also an excellent way to use cold turkey on Boxing Day. If chicory is not available, celery may be used instead.

1 × 1 1/2 kg (3–3 1/2 lb) cooked chicken
4 heads chicory
3 dessert apples
2 tablespoons lemon juice
50 g (2 oz) sultanas
2 oranges
1–2 grapefruit (depending on size)
300 ml (10 fl oz) low-fat natural yogurt
A little paprika, to garnish

1. Remove all skin and fat from the chicken. Free the flesh from the bones and cut into finger-length strips.
2. Wash the chicory under cold running water and drain well. Do not leave to soak as this will make it bitter. Slice two heads into thin rings. Break the other two heads into separate leaves.
3. Peel, core and dice the apples. Place in a bowl with the lemon juice and mix well.
4. Wash and drain the sultanas, place in a bowl

and cover with boiling water. Leave to stand for 5 minutes, then drain well.

5. Grate the zest from one of the oranges and reserve. Using a small serrated knife, cut the peel and pith from both oranges and the grapefruit, then cut out the segments from between the membranes.

6. Mix the chicken with the chicory rings, diced apple and sultanas. Add the grated orange zest to the yogurt and stir into the chicken mixture. Season to taste, adding a little caster sugar if you wish.

7. Arrange the leaves of chicory decoratively at each end of the dish and pile the chicken mixture into the middle. Arrange the orange and grapefruit segments around the edge of the dish and sprinkle a little paprika over the chicken. Refrigerate until served.

Suggested Vegetables
Green salad.

TURKEY ESCALOPES WITH GRAND MARNIER
ESCALOPES DE DINDE AU GRAND MARNIER
SERVES 4
Cooking time: 30–40 minutes

4 × 100 g (4 oz) turkey escalopes (thin slices of turkey breasts beaten flat)
Salt
Freshly ground black pepper
2 oranges
1 lemon
150 ml (5 fl oz) chicken stock
150 ml (5 fl oz) dry white wine or cider
2 tablespoons Grand Marnier or other orange liqueur
1 tablespoon chopped fresh chervil or parsley

1. Place the escalopes in a heatproof casserole or frying pan and season with salt and freshly ground black pepper.

2. Grate the zest of one orange. Squeeze the juice from this orange and the lemon. Cut the other orange into slices and cut each slice in half.

3. Pour the stock, white wine or cider, orange and lemon juice over the turkey. Add the grated orange zest. Bring gently to the boil, cover and simmer gently for 30–40 minutes until the turkey is tender.

4. Place the escalopes on a hot serving dish, cover and keep hot.

5. Add the Grand Marnier or other orange liqueur to the sauce. Bring to the boil and, if necessary, boil rapidly until reduced to a coating consistency. Pour over the escalopes.

6. Arrange the half slices of orange around the edge of the dish. Sprinkle chopped fresh chervil or parsley over the top just before serving. Serve hot.

Microwave
The turkey escalopes can be microwaved on a low setting. Reduce the sauce according to the recipe.

Suggested Vegetables
Braised Fennel or Celery (page 89), French beans, spinach or peas, Orange Rice Pilaff (page 93) or Hip and Thigh Duchess Potatoes (page 95).

Janet Farrar wrote:

'I have been teaching dance and exercise classes for some years, and in spite of all the exercise I do and have done, I have never been able to reduce my enormous thighs significantly – until now. I intend following the diet and maintenance programme and spreading the good word to as many people as possible!

P.S. I am a whole dress size smaller now! Wonderful!'

Turkey, Pineapple and Pasta Salad
SERVES 4–6

This is another excellent recipe to use with leftover turkey at Christmas or for a buffet party. Fusilli are the short twisted lengths of pasta but you can choose any shape you like. Wholewheat pasta can also be used.

450 g (1 lb) cooked turkey meat
2 tablespoons lemon juice
1 teaspoon paprika (page 60)
175 g (6 oz) fusilli or other egg-free pasta
175 g (6 oz) celery
4–5 tablespoons low-fat fromage frais or yogurt
2–3 tablespoons tomato ketchup
1 ½ tablespoons horseradish relish
1 × 225 g (8 oz) can pineapple pieces in natural juice
Salt
Freshly ground black pepper
1 lettuce
A little extra paprika, to garnish

1. Remove the skin from the turkey and cut into bite-sized pieces. Mix with the lemon juice and paprika, cover and refrigerate for about 1 hour.
2. Meanwhile, place the pasta in a pan of boiling salted water and cook until just tender. Drain. Rinse under cold running water until completely cold. Drain well.
3. Trim, wash and slice the celery.
4. Mix the fromage frais with the tomato ketchup and the horseradish relish.
5. Drain the pineapple pieces. Stir into the sauce with the pasta and the turkey. Season to taste with salt and freshly ground black pepper.
6. Wash and drain the lettuce. Arrange the leaves around the edge of a serving dish. Pile the turkey mixture into the centre and sprinkle a little paprika over the top. Refrigerate until served.

Glazed Duck Breasts with Cherry Sauce
SERVES 4
Cooking time: 18–20 minutes
Oven: 220°C, 425°F (Gas Mark 7)

Dark Morello cherries are best for this dish. They are an English variety of cooking cherry and are usually available in the UK from mid-June to the end of July. However cherries can be pickled (page 79) and used throughout the year. Look out for Bradbourne Black and Gauchers. They are English dark dessert cherries – ideal for pickling as well as eating fresh. Other imported cherries are quite suitable but they are more expensive.

If you use pickled cherries in this recipe, leave the wine vinegar out of the sauce and, if necessary, add a little when you have tasted it. Canned and bottled cherries can also be used but drain well and marinate them in the wine vinegar for an hour or two before you use them, to counteract the sweetness from the syrup. Frozen cherries can be used in the same way as fresh ones.

4 × 175–225 g (6–8 oz) duck breasts
2 tablespoons redcurrant jelly
¼ teaspoon ground cinnamon
A good pinch freshly ground nutmeg
175 g (6 oz) dark sour cherries (see introduction above)
½ teaspoon French mustard
2 tablespoons dark soy sauce
1 tablespoon red wine vinegar
150 ml (5 fl oz) chicken stock
1 heaped teaspoon arrowroot
A few sprigs watercress, to garnish

1. Remove the skin and fat from the duck breasts. (You will find that it pulls off very easily.) With a sharp knife, remove any sinews from the underside.
2. Warm the redcurrant jelly in a pan and stir in

the cinnamon and nutmeg. Taste and add a little more cinnamon or nutmeg if you wish.

3. Place the duck breasts in a roasting tin and glaze with the redcurrant jelly, reserving the residue of the jelly. Cook in a preheated oven at 220°C, 425°F (Gas Mark 7) for 18–20 minutes until the duck is tender but still slightly pink in the centre.

4. Meanwhile, stone the cherries and place them in the pan containing the residue of the redcurrant jelly. Add the French mustard, dark soy sauce, red wine vinegar and stock. Bring to the boil and cook gently for 6–8 minutes until the cherries are just tender. Mix the arrowroot with a little water, add to the pan and bring to the boil, stirring all the time. Tinned cherries need only be heated through in the sauce but a little more arrowroot may be required to thicken it.

5. When the duck breasts are cooked, cut each one in 1 cm (½ inch) slices along the length almost down to the base, and fan out. Arrange the four breasts in a semi-circle on a hot serving dish. Just before serving, use a slotted spoon to remove the cherries from the sauce and pile them at the bottom of the duck breasts. Pour a little sauce over each one and serve the rest of the sauce separately. Garnish the top edge of the dish with small sprigs of watercress.

Microwave
Do not microwave.

Suggested Vegetables
Mange-tout (page 90), French beans, broccoli, courgettes, new potatoes, Dry-roast Potatoes (page 94) or Hip and Thigh Duchess Potatoes (page 95).

PICKLED CHERRIES

This quantity is sufficient to fill a 1 litre (1¾ pint) jar or container. Choose one with a tight-fitting lid. Preserving jars are ideal for this but make sure that the vinegar does not touch any metal in the lid. These cherries can be served as a garnish or a pickle with duck, pork, ham and all red meats.

1 kg (2 lb) dark cherries (page 78)
450 g (1 lb) granulated sugar
750 ml (1¼ pints) red wine vinegar
2 cloves
1 bay leaf
1 × 5 cm (2 inches) piece cinnamon stick

1. Wash the cherries, drain and dry well on kitchen paper or a tea towel. Remove the stalks and cut a cross on the top of each cherry. Place in a clean dry jar.

2. Put the sugar, red wine vinegar, cloves, bay leaf and cinnamon stick in a pan. Bring to the boil, stirring all the time. Allow the sugar to dissolve before the liquid reaches boiling point. Boil for 5 minutes. Then leave to stand until cool. Pour the liquid over the cherries.

3. Seal so that they are air-tight and store for 6 weeks before serving.

GUINEA FOWL WITH GRAPES
PINTADE À LA VIGNERONNE
SERVES 4
Cooking time: 1–1 ¼ hours
Oven: 180°C, 350°F (Gas Mark 4)

Great care needs to be taken with the seasoning of this dish. The sauce is reduced at the end of the cooking time and if too much seasoning is added to begin with, it becomes very salty. For this reason, if using a stock cube to make the stock, use only half the normal quantity.

1 × 1.75 kg (3½ lb) guinea fowl
1 carrot
1 onion
2 sticks celery
300 ml (10 fl oz) dry white wine
300 ml (10 fl oz) chicken stock
2–3 parsley stalks
1 bay leaf
1 sprig fresh thyme
5–6 juniper berries
Salt
Freshly ground black pepper
225 g (8 oz) white grapes (preferably seedless)
1 tablespoon chopped fresh parsley

1. Truss the guinea fowl or ask your butcher to do this for you.
2. Peel and slice the carrot and onion. Trim, wash and slice the celery.
3. Place the vegetables in the base of a deep heatproof casserole. Place the guinea fowl on top, pour on the white wine and stock, and tuck the parsley stalks, bay leaf, fresh thyme and juniper berries down the side. Season lightly with salt and freshly ground black pepper. Bring to the boil, cover and transfer to a preheated oven at 180°C, 350°F (Gas Mark 4) for 1–1 ¼ hours until the bird is tender.
4. If seedless grapes are not available, remove the grape pips. A new hairgrip is ideal for this.
5. When the guinea fowl is cooked, transfer it

to a hot serving dish and remove the trussing strings. Keep hot.
6. Strain the cooking liquor into a pan and bring to the boil. Use a tablespoon to remove any scum which rises to the surface. (This is the fat which has seeped from the bird.) Boil the sauce rapidly until it starts to become syrupy. Add the grapes and cook for a moment to two longer. Add the chopped fresh parsley and check the seasoning.
7. Using a slotted spoon, remove the grapes from the sauce and pile them at each end of the serving dish. Pour over some of the sauce and serve the rest separately. Serve hot.

Microwave
The guinea fowl can be microwaved but reduce the sauce according to the recipe.

Suggested Vegetables
French or runner beans, carrots, broccoli, Brussels sprouts or spinach, Orange Rice Pilaff (page 93), new potatoes or Hip and Thigh Duchess Potatoes (page 95).

Guinea Fowl with Grapes (p. 80), Pears Aurora (p. 106)

BRAISED PIGEONS
(Maintenance Diet dinner only)
SERVES 4
Cooking time: 1½–1¾ hours
Oven: 180°C, 350°F (Gas Mark 4)

If pigeons are unavailable, quail may be used in this recipe.

350 g (12 oz) pickling onions
2–3 carrots
1 clove garlic or ½ teaspoon garlic paste
75–100 g (3–4 oz) lean back bacon or gammon steak
100 g (4 oz) button mushrooms
A good pinch dried thyme
A good pinch dried marjoram
1 sprig rosemary or a pinch dried rosemary
2 tablespoons chopped fresh parsley
200 ml (7 fl oz) chicken stock
200 ml (7 fl oz) red wine, dry white wine or cider
1 tablespoon tomato purée
Salt
Freshly ground black pepper
4 pigeons, drawn and trussed
175 g (16 oz) frozen peas
1–1½ teaspoons arrowroot (optional)

1. Peel the onions, carrots and fresh garlic. Dice the carrots and crush the garlic. Remove the rind and any fat from the bacon or gammon and cut into strips.
2. Wipe, trim and cut the mushrooms into quarters.

3. Place the onions, carrots and bacon or gammon in a heatproof casserole. Add the herbs and stir in the chicken stock, red or white wine or cider and tomato purée. Season to taste with salt and freshly ground black pepper. Place the pigeons on top, cover and bring to the boil. Transfer to a preheated oven at 180°C, 350°F (Gas Mark 4) and cook for 1½–1¾ hours until tender. Add the mushrooms and peas about 15 minutes before the end of the cooking time.
4. When the pigeons are tender, lift them out of the pan, remove the trussing strings and place on a hot deep dish. Keep hot.
5. If you wish, you can now thicken the sauce. Strain the cooking liquor into a pan and keep the vegetables on one side. Use 1 teaspoon arrowroot for each 300 ml (10 fl oz) liquid. Mix the arrowroot with a little water, add to the pan and bring to the boil, stirring all the time. Return the vegetables to the sauce. Reheat and check the seasoning. Pour around the pigeons and serve hot.

Microwave
Can be cooked in a microwave but reduce liquid to 150 ml (5 fl oz) stock and 150 ml (5 fl oz) wine or cider.

Suggested Vegetables
Cabbage, Brussels sprouts or other green vegetables. Jacket or boiled potatoes or Lentil Roast (page 92).

Peach Ambrosia (p. 106), Glazed Duck Breasts with Cherry Sauce (p. 78), Chicory and Orange Salad (p. 31)

BASQUE RABBIT
LAPIN À LA BASQUAISE
SERVES 4
Soaking time: 1 hour
Cooking time: 1½–2 hours
Oven: 160°C, 325°F (Gas Mark 3)

1 × 1¼–1½ kg (2½–3 lb) rabbit or 1 kg (2 lb)
 rabbit joints (approximate weight)
100 g (4 oz) mushrooms
1 onion
2 cloves garlic or 1 teaspoon garlic paste
1 green pepper
300 ml (10 fl oz) tomato passata (page 97), or
 1 × 400 g (14 oz) can tomatoes and
 1 tablespoon tomato purée
200 ml (7 fl oz) dry white wine or cider
1 tablespoon chopped fresh parsley
½ teaspoon dried thyme
Salt
Freshly ground black pepper
Extra chopped fresh parsley, to garnish

1. Joint the rabbit, if necessary, or ask your butcher to do this for you. Soak the joints in cold salted water for 1 hour.
2. Meanwhile, trim, wipe and slice the mushrooms. Peel the onion and fresh garlic. Slice the onion and crush the garlic. Remove the stalk, pith and seeds from the pepper and cut into dice.
3. Rinse and drain the rabbit joints and place all the ingredients in a heatproof casserole. Season to taste with salt and freshly ground black pepper. Cover and bring to the boil. Transfer to a preheated oven at 160°C, 325°F (Gas Mark 3) for 1½–2 hours until tender.
4. Check the seasoning, pour into a hot serving dish and sprinkle extra chopped fresh parsley over the top just before serving. Serve hot.

Microwave
Reduce the amount of passata by one-third or leave out 150 ml (5 fl oz) juice from the can of tomatoes. Then microwave on a low setting.

Add extra liquid, if necessary, during the cooking time.

Suggested Vegetables
Carrots, cabbage, Braised Fennel or Celery (page 89), new or creamed potatoes (made with skimmed milk or low-fat natural yogurt).

Janet Lea wrote:

'I would like to say a very big thank you for giving me the inspiration to do something about my shape. I have always had a very definite pear shape throughout my life, and a big bottom which has always made me most unhappy. As I got older (I am 42) I found it increasingly difficult to diet and very often when trying to reduce my calorie intake, found I felt quite nauseous and not able to continue a diet for more than a couple of days.

I read an article on Rosemary Conley and was inspired by what appeared to be a kindred spirit. I thought I would give this diet my once-and-for-all best shot. To my surprise I found it easy to follow, most enjoyable, and was not hungry at all.

Because I have a job as a secretary which naturally means sitting down a lot, I am amazed at how the cellulite has gone. My thighs are quite smooth in comparison to before and I would not now hesitate to wear shorts or a swimming costume without constantly pulling down the legs to hide my lumpy thighs. I feel and look more attractive and I am very happy with my new shape.'

RABBIT WITH PRUNES
LAPIN AUX PRUNEAUX
SERVES 4
Marinading time: Overnight
Cooking time: 1½–2 hours
Oven: 160°C, 325°F (Gas Mark 3)

---

1 × 1¼–1½ kg (2½–3 lb) rabbit or 1 kg (2 lb)
*   rabbit joints (approximate weight)*
2 carrots
1 large onion
3 cloves garlic or 1½ teaspoons garlic paste
450 ml (¾ pint) red wine, or 225 ml (7½ fl oz)
*   red wine and 225 ml (7½ fl oz) chicken stock*
2 tablespoons brandy (optional)
1 bay leaf
2–3 parsley stalks
1 sprig fresh thyme
10 black peppercorns
Salt
225 g (8 oz) small pickling onions
100 g (4 oz) lean bacon steak or gammon steak
20–24 prunes
1–2 teaspoons arrowroot (optional)

1. Joint the rabbit, if necessary, or ask your butcher to do this for you. Soak the joints in cold salted water for 1 hour.
2. Peel and slice the carrots, onion and fresh garlic.
3. Place the rabbit in a deep dish with the carrots, onion and garlic. Add the red wine, brandy (if used), bay leaf, parsley stalks, fresh thyme and black peppercorns. Cover and refrigerate until the next day, turning the rabbit in the marinade occasionally.
4. To cook the rabbit, place in a deep heatproof casserole with the vegetables, herbs, wine from the marinade, and the stock (if used). Season with salt, cover and bring to the boil. Transfer to a preheated oven at 160°C, 325°F (Gas Mark 3) and cook for 1½–2 hours until the rabbit is tender.
5. Meanwhile, carefully peel the pickling onions, leaving the root and stem ends intact so that the

centres do not pop out while they are being cooked.
6. Cut the bacon or gammon into 1 cm (½ inch) dice. Pour boiling water on to the prunes and leave to stand for 1 hour.
7. Halfway through the cooking time add the onions and bacon.
8. Fifteen minutes before the end of the cooking time, drain the prunes, remove the stones if you wish, and add the prunes to the casserole.
9. To serve, use a slotted spoon to transfer the rabbit, vegetables and prunes to a hot serving dish, removing the bay leaf, parsley stalks, thyme and peppercorns. If you wish to thicken the sauce, measure the cooking liquor and use 1 teaspoon arrowroot to every 300 ml (10 fl oz) liquid. Mix the arrowroot with a little water, add to the cooking liquor and bring to the boil, stirring all the time. Check the seasoning and pour over the rabbit. Serve hot.

Microwave
Can be microwaved on a low setting but thicken the sauce, if necessary, according to the recipe.

Suggested Vegetables
French or green beans, carrots, Brussels sprouts or broccoli, new potatoes or Hip and Thigh Duchess Potatoes (page 95).

SALADS AND VEGETABLES

Did you ever think you would be able to eat chips on a diet? Well, you can if you cook them my way. So little oil is used that anyone – both Hip and Thigh and Maintenance Dieters – can eat them (in reasonable amounts).

Many of the salads make delicious lunchtime meals and vegetarians should find several appealing recipes.

Steaming (page 96) is an excellent way to cook vegetables for the Hip and Thigh Diet. All the flavour and goodness of the vegetables is retained and, because they are not cooked in the water itself, they stay firm. (This is particularly good for courgettes and marrows which can become mushy when cooked in water.) Steaming is also economical as the steamer can often be placed over pans cooking something else.

WATERCRESS AND ORANGE SALAD
SERVES 4–6

2 bunches watercress
2 oranges
1–2 tablespoons white wine vinegar
Salt
Freshly ground black pepper

1. Wash and pick over the watercress. Discard any very thick stems and break large pieces of watercress into smaller ones.
2. Grate the zest of one orange and reserve.
3. Using a small serrated knife, cut the peel and pith from both oranges and then cut out the segments from between the membranes. Do this over a plate so that any juice is kept.
4. Squeeze the juice from the membranes and core. Pour into a bowl with the rest of the juice. Add the grated orange zest and sufficient white wine vinegar to your taste. Season well with salt and freshly ground black pepper.
5. Cut the orange segments into two or three pieces. Mix in a salad bowl with the watercress, pour over the dressing and toss well before serving.

TOMATO AND KIWI SALAD
SERVES 4–6

This salad is an excellent accompaniment to cold chicken or fish dishes.

450 g (1 lb) medium-sized tomatoes
2–3 kiwi fruit
3–4 tablespoons Oil-free Vinaigrette (page 112)
Salt
Freshly ground black pepper
Chopped fresh parsley or chives, to garnish

1. With a small sharp knife, remove the small piece of hard core in the stalk end of each tomato. Skin (page 97) and slice the tomatoes and peel and slice the kiwi fruit.
2. Starting with tomatoes on the outer edge, arrange the tomato and kiwi slices in alternate overlapping circles on a round flat dish.
3. Pour over the vinaigrette, season with salt and freshly ground black pepper, and sprinkle some chopped fresh parsley or chives over the top.
4. Cover and refrigerate until served.

COLESLAW
SERVES 4–6

175–225 g (6–8 oz) white cabbage
2 medium-sized carrots
1 small leek or 3–4 spring onions
150 ml (5 fl oz) low-fat natural yogurt
1 teaspoon French mustard
Salt
Freshly ground black pepper
A little caster sugar or artificial sweetener
  (optional)

1. Wash and finely shred the cabbage. Drain well.
2. Peel and coarsely grate the carrots.
3. Trim and wash the leek or spring onions. Discard the dark-green part of the leek. Slice very thinly.
4. To make the dressing, mix the yogurt with the French mustard and season to taste with salt and freshly ground black pepper. Add a little caster sugar or sweetener if you wish.
5. Mix the vegetables together in a salad bowl and stir in the dressing.
6. Cover and refrigerate until served.

SPICY SALAD
SERVES 4–6

Many supermarkets now sell a variety of lettuces from France and Italy. They come in different colours and textures and help to add variety to your salads. Some are dark red like Radicchio from Italy or the Feuille de Chêne lettuce from France. (In English this is called Oak Leaf lettuce but it is usually found labelled under its French name.) One of the most usual curly lettuces is the pale wispy Frisée or Curly Endive. The Italians also grow some attractive curly lettuce. There is the red-tinged Lollo Rosso or the pale-green Lollo Biondi.

To make this salad really interesting mix some red-leafed lettuce with a curly one or a crisp Webb's Wonder. Because lettuces vary so much in size, no quantity is given – just use as much as you need.

I lettuce (see introduction above)
175 g (6 oz) celery
½ green pepper
2 medium-sized onions
65 ml (2½ fl oz) white wine vinegar or cider
    vinegar
¼ teaspoon French mustard
A few drops Tabasco sauce
I teaspoon paprika (page 60)
Salt
Caster sugar or artificial sweetener to taste

1. Wash and drain the lettuce. Break the leaves into small pieces.
2. Wash and trim the celery, remove the stalk, pith and seeds from the pepper and peel the onions.
3. Finely chop or grate the vegetables on a coarse grater.
4. Blend the vinegar, mustard, Tabasco sauce and paprika together. Season with salt and caster sugar or sweetener to taste.
5. Mix the lettuce and grated vegetables

together in a salad bowl and pour over the dressing just before serving. Toss well.

CELERY, FRUIT AND YOGURT SALAD
SERVES 4–6

Oranges, tinned mandarins (in natural juice) or grapefruit can be used instead of clementines, or, if you prefer, you could use an assortment of these fruits. This salad can also be served as an hors-d'oeuvre.

I small head of celery
2 clementines
3 small dessert apples
150 ml (5 fl oz) low-fat natural yogurt
I tablespoon lemon juice
Salt
Freshly ground black pepper
¼ teaspoon caraway seeds (optional)
I small lettuce

1. Wash and trim the celery. Reserve the leaves from the heart and slice the rest.
2. Peel the clementines and remove the white membranes from each segment.
3. Peel the apples, cut into quarters, remove the cores and dice.
4. Mix the yogurt with the lemon juice. Season to taste with salt and freshly ground black pepper, and add the caraway seeds (if used).
5. Stir the celery, clementine segments and diced apples into the yogurt mixture. Mix well.
6. Wash, drain and dry the lettuce and line a salad bowl with the leaves. Pile the celery, fruit and yogurt mixture into the centre. Garnish with the reserved celery leaves. Cover and refrigerate until served.

MIXED BEAN SALAD
SERVES 4–6

Any mixture of beans can be used for this dish. Tinned ones have been used here for convenience but if you prefer you can cook your own. If you cook your own red kidney beans please follow the instructions on page 38. Chickpeas or sweetcorn can also be used.

213 g (7½ oz) can butter beans
213 g (7½ oz) can red kidney beans
213 g (7½ oz) can black-eyed beans or flagolet beans
1 onion
2 sticks celery
3 tablespoons apple juice or cider
1 tablespoon lemon juice
1 tablespoon white wine vinegar or cider vinegar
½ teaspoon French mustard
Salt
Freshly ground black pepper
Chopped fresh chives, to garnish

1. Drain the beans, wash quickly under cold running water and drain well again.
2. Peel and thinly slice the onion and break the slices into rings. Trim, wash and dice the celery.
3. To make the dressing, mix the apple juice or cider with the lemon juice, vinegar, and French mustard. Whisk well and season to taste with salt and freshly ground black pepper.
4. Mix the beans, onion rings and celery together in a salad bowl. Pour over the dressing and toss well. Sprinkle the chopped fresh chives over the top.
5. Cover and refrigerate until served.

CUCUMBER AND YOGURT SALAD
SERVES 4

This tangy cucumber salad comes from the Middle East. It is often eaten as an hors-d'oeuvre in Greece and can also be served as an accompaniment to curry. If you wish, you can peel the cucumber but the salad will lose some of its colour.

½ medium-sized cucumber
Salt
1 clove garlic or ½ teaspoon garlic paste
150 ml (5 fl oz) low-fat natural yogurt
1 tablespoon chopped fresh mint
Salt
Freshly ground black pepper

1. Peel the cucumber if you wish. Dice roughly and sprinkle a little salt over and leave to stand for 30–40 minutes. Rinse well under cold running water. Drain and dry well on kitchen paper.
2. Peel and crush the fresh garlic.
3. Place the cucumber in a bowl with the yogurt, garlic and chopped fresh mint. Mix well and season to taste with salt and freshly ground black pepper.
4. Cover and refrigerate until well chilled before serving.

right, Mixed Bean Salad (p. 88), Cucumber and Yogurt Salad (p. 88), Celery, Fruit and Yogurt Salad (p. 87); overleaf, Turkey, Pineapple and Pasta Salad (p. 78), Watercress and Orange Salad (p. 86), Chicken and Chicory Salad (p. 76)

BRAISED FENNEL
SERVES 4–6
Cooking time: 1–1 ¼ hours
Oven: 200°C, 400°F (Gas Mark 6)

The fennel used in this recipe is different from the herb of the same name. It looks like a bulbous celery and has a slight aniseed flavour. Cooked in this way it can be served hot as a vegetable dish or cold as an hors-d'oeuvre. Celery can be cooked in the same way and served hot.

2–3 bulbs fennel
1 onion
1 clove garlic or ½ teaspoon garlic paste
350 g (12 oz) tomatoes
150 ml (5 fl oz) vegetable or chicken stock
Salt
Freshly ground black pepper
Chopped fresh parsley, to garnish

1. Wash the fennel and cut off any damaged parts. Cut each bulb into quarters. Blanch in boiling salted water for 15 minutes.
2. Meanwhile, peel the onion and fresh garlic. Finely chop the onion and crush the garlic. Skin (page 97) the tomatoes and cut into quarters.
3. Drain the fennel and place in an ovenproof casserole with the onion, tomatoes and garlic. Heat the stock and pour over. Season lightly with salt and freshly ground black pepper. Cover and cook in a preheated oven at 200°C, 400°F (Gas Mark 6) for 1–1 ¼ hours until the fennel is tender.
4. Check the seasoning and serve hot or cold. Sprinkle the chopped fresh parsley over the top just before serving.

left, Lentil Roast (p. 92), French Country-style Peas (p. 90), Leeks Niçoise (p. 89); previous page, Italian Cauliflower (p. 92), Broccoli with Tomatoes and Mushrooms (p. 91), Braised Fennel (p. 89)

LEEKS NIÇOISE
SERVES 4–6
Cooking time: 10–15 minutes

This dish can also be served as an hors-d'oeuvre.

1 kg (2 lb) small leeks
225 g (8 oz) small ripe tomatoes
1 clove garlic or ½ teaspoon garlic paste
1 lemon
Salt
Freshly ground black pepper
1 tablespoon chopped fresh parsley

1. Trim and wash the leeks well and cut into pieces approximately 7.5 cm (3 inches) long. Cook in a pan of boiling salted water for 10–15 minutes until the leeks are just tender but still hold their shape.
2. Meanwhile, skin (page 97) the tomatoes and cut into quarters. Peel and crush the fresh garlic. Grate the zest from the lemon and reserve. Squeeze the juice.
3. Place the lemon juice in a non-stick frying pan with the garlic and tomatoes. Season to taste with salt and freshly ground black pepper. Cover and cook until the tomatoes are just tender but still hold their shape. Stir in the chopped fresh parsley. Check the seasoning and leave until cool.
4. When the leeks are cooked, drain well and rinse under cold running water until they are completely cold. Drain well in a colander, then place on kitchen paper until they are absolutely dry.
5. Arrange the leeks on a serving dish. Pour over the tomato mixture and sprinkle the grated lemon zest over the top. Refrigerate until served.

FRENCH COUNTRY-STYLE PEAS
SERVES 4
Cooking time: 25–30 minutes

This dish is nicest cooked with fresh peas but if you want to use frozen ones, add them about 5 minutes before the end of the cooking time. You can easily adjust the quantities to cater for any number of people but try to use equal quantities of each vegetable.

8 pickling onions
8 small carrots (preferably new ones)
8–12 small new potatoes
1 small lettuce
250 g (8 oz) fresh shelled peas
300 ml (10 fl oz) chicken or vegetable stock
Salt
Freshly ground black pepper
½–1 teaspoon arrowroot
Chopped fresh parsley or chervil, to garnish

1. Peel the onions, leaving the root and stem ends intact so that the centres do not pop out while they are being cooked. Scrape the carrots and potatoes. If necessary, cut the carrots in half.
2. Trim and wash the lettuce, keeping it whole. Then cut into quarters.
3. Place all the vegetables (including the fresh peas) in a pan. Pour on the stock, season lightly with salt and freshly ground black pepper, and bring to the boil. Cover and simmer gently for 25–30 minutes until all the vegetables are tender.
4. Drain the vegetables, reserving the cooking liquor, and pile them into a hot serving dish. Cover and keep hot.
5. Measure the cooking liquor and allow ½ teaspoon arrowroot for each 150 ml (5 fl oz) liquid. Mix the arrowroot with a little water. Return the cooking liquor to the pan and add the arrowroot. Bring to the boil, stirring all the time. Check the seasoning and pour over the vegetables. Sprinkle the chopped fresh parsley or chervil over the top just before serving. Serve hot.

MANGE-TOUT
(Snow peas)
Cooking time: 5–8 minutes

Although mange-tout seem expensive, they go a long way because there is little waste. They are nicer when still slightly crisp, so don't overcook them. The exact cooking time will depend on freshness and size – test them until they are just the way you like them. Cook them at the last moment so that you can take them straight to the table.

About 225 g (8 oz) will be sufficient for four people if you are serving other vegetables. They are easy to grow but don't plant too many at once as the pods need to be cooked when very young. If you sow them in small batches you can have a supply throughout the summer.

225 g (8 oz) mange-tout
Salt
Freshly ground black pepper

1. Wash, top and tail the mange-tout and remove the strings from the edges.
2. Place in a pan of boiling salted water and cook for 5–8 minutes until just tender. Drain well, pile into a hot serving dish and season to taste with a little salt, if necessary, and freshly ground black pepper.

BROCCOLI WITH TOMATOES AND MUSHROOMS
SERVES 4–6
Cooking time: 15–20 minutes

450–750 g (1–1½ lb) broccoli
1 onion
1 clove garlic or ½ teaspoon garlic paste
450 g (1 lb) large ripe tomatoes or 400 g (14 oz)
   can chopped tomatoes
A pinch caster sugar or artificial sweetener
Salt
Freshly ground black pepper
100 g (4 oz) small button mushrooms
1–2 teaspoons lemon juice
Chopped fresh parsley, to garnish

1. Wash the broccoli and cut it into small florets. Cut the stems quite short and slit them if they are thick.
2. Peel the onion and fresh garlic. Finely chop the onion and crush the garlic. Skin (page 97), de-seed and chop the fresh tomatoes.
3. Place the tomatoes, onion, garlic and caster sugar in a heavy-based pan with 1–2 tablespoons water or the juice from the canned tomatoes. Season with salt and freshly ground black pepper and cook for 15–20 minutes or until the onion is tender. Add a little more water, if necessary, to prevent the mixture sticking to the bottom of the pan. Add the sweetener, if used.
4. Meanwhile, wipe, trim and slice the mushrooms. Place in a pan with the lemon juice and 1–2 tablespoons water. Season lightly and cook for 5–8 minutes until the mushrooms are tender and the liquid has evaporated. Stir into the tomato mixture.
5. While the mushrooms are cooking, place the broccoli spears in a pan of boiling salted water and cook for 8–10 minutes until just tender. Drain well.
6. Arrange most of the broccoli around the edge of a hot round plate. Reheat the tomato mixture, if necessary, and pour it in a ring inside the broccoli. Place the rest of the broccoli neatly in the centre.
7. Sprinkle the chopped fresh parsley over the top just before serving. Serve hot.

CARROTS IN YOGURT
SERVES 4–6
Cooking time: 12–18 minutes

450–750 g (1–1½ lb) carrots
A pinch freshly grated nutmeg
50 g (2 oz) sultanas
150 ml (5 fl oz) low-fat natural yogurt
Salt
Freshly ground black pepper
A little caster sugar (optional)
Chopped fresh chervil or parsley, to garnish

1. Peel the carrots and slice thinly. Place in a pan of boiling salted water and cook for 10–15 minutes until tender.
2. Meanwhile, place the sultanas in a small bowl and cover with boiling water.
3. Drain the carrots and sultanas well. Return the carrots to the pan and stir in the nutmeg, sultanas and yogurt. Season to taste with salt and freshly ground black pepper and add a little caster sugar if you wish. Reheat gently but do not allow to boil.
4. Pile into a hot serving dish and sprinkle the chopped fresh chervil or parsley over the top just before serving. Serve hot.

LENTIL ROAST
SERVES 3–4
as a main meal; 4–6 as an accompaniment
Cooking time:
Boiling 20–30 minutes
Roasting 1 hour
Oven: 180°C, 350°F (Gas Mark 4)

Served with an assortment of other vegetables, this dish makes an excellent vegetarian meal. It can also be served as an accompaniment to roast and boiled meats, particularly pork and ham, instead of potatoes.

350 g (12 oz) orange lentils
1 bay leaf
2–3 parsley stalks
1 sprig fresh thyme
2 large onions
1–2 cloves garlic or 1/2–1 teaspoon garlic paste
2–3 sticks celery
1/2 green pepper
1/2 red pepper
1 dessert apple
75 g (3 oz) plain, low-fat quark or yogurt
Salt
Freshly ground black pepper

1. Wash the lentils well, drain and place in a large pan. Cover with water. (Do not add salt at this stage.) Tie the bay leaf, parsley stalks and thyme together with string and add to the pan. Bring to the boil.
2. Peel the onions and fresh garlic. Chop the onion and crush the garlic. Wash, trim and slice the celery. Add the onions, garlic and celery to the lentils and simmer until the lentils and vegetables are tender and the liquid has almost evaporated.
3. Meanwhile, remove the pith and seeds from the peppers. Peel the apple, cut into quarters and remove the core. Cut both the peppers and apple into small dice.
4. When the lentils are tender, remove the bunch of herbs and continue cooking, stirring all

the time until the mixture is quite dry. Stir in the peppers and apples with the quark. Mix well and season to taste with salt and freshly ground black pepper.
5. Pile the mixture into an ovenproof dish and bake in a preheated oven at 180°C, 350°F (Gas Mark 4) for about 1 hour until the top is springy like a sponge.
6. Serve hot with a selection of vegetables in season.

ITALIAN CAULIFLOWER
CHOUFLEUR ITALIENNE
SERVES 4
Cooking time:
Cauliflower 12–15 minutes
Sauce 25–30 minutes

---

1 quantity Tomato Sauce (page 113)
1 cauliflower
2–3 tablespoons browned breadcrumbs
A little Parmesan cheese (Maintenance Dieters only)

1. Make the Tomato Sauce (page 113).
2. Wash and trim the cauliflower. Break into large florets, place in a pan of boiling salted water and cook for 12–15 minutes until just tender. Drain and place on a hot serving dish.
3. Heat the Tomato Sauce and pour over the cauliflower. Sprinkle the breadcrumbs over the top just before serving.
4. Maintenance Dieters can serve a little Parmesan cheese separately to sprinkle (sparsely) over the top.

CUCUMBER WITH SAGE
SERVES 4
Cooking time: 15–20 minutes

In Great Britain, we rarely think of cooking cucumber but it is often served in France and is well worth trying because it has a delicious delicate flavour. It is excellent with grilled or baked fish.

1 large cucumber
Salt
150 ml (5 fl oz) low-fat natural yogurt
2 teaspoons chopped fresh sage or 1 teaspoon dried sage
1 tablespoon chopped fresh parsley
Freshly ground black pepper

1. Wash but do not peel the cucumber. Cut into 1 cm (½ inch) dice. Sprinkle over a little salt and leave to stand for 20 minutes. Take care not to over-salt; more can be added later.
2. Rinse the cucumber and place in a pan with 2–3 tablespoons water. Cover and cook over a gentle heat for 15–20 minutes until the cucumber is tender and the water has evaporated.
3. Stir in the yogurt and most of the sage and parsley. Season with freshly ground black pepper and more salt, if necessary.
4. Reheat gently without boiling. Pile into a hot serving dish and sprinkle the rest of the herbs over the top just before serving. Serve hot.

ORANGE RICE PILAFF
SERVES 4–6
Cooking time: 12–15 minutes

This fragrant savoury rice dish can be served with kebabs, fish or chicken dishes.

3 oranges
1 onion
12 cardamom pods
100–175 g (4–6 oz) long-grain rice
¼ teaspoon turmeric
450–600 ml (15 fl oz–1 pt) chicken stock
Salt
White pepper

1. Grate the zest and squeeze the juice from two oranges. With a potato peeler, cut the peel very thinly from the third orange, making certain that there is no pith on it as this will be bitter. Cut into very thin strips. Blanch the strips in boiling salted water for 3–4 minutes, then drain and chill under cold running water. Drain well again and reserve.
2. Peel and finely chop the onion.
3. Bruise the cardamom pods with a rolling pin.
4. Place the rice in a pan with the grated orange zest, orange juice, onion, cardamom pods and turmeric. Add the stock and season with salt and white pepper. Bring to the boil, cover and cook until the rice and onions are tender and all the liquid has been absorbed. Check the seasoning.
5. Pile the rice into a hot serving dish and sprinkle the strips of orange peel over the top just before serving.

DRY-ROAST PARSNIPS
SERVES 3–4
Cooking time: 30–45 minutes
Oven: 200°C, 400°F (Gas Mark 6)

4–6 medium parsnips
Salt

1. Peel and halve the parsnips. Place in a pan of cold salted water, bring to the boil and blanch for 5 minutes.
2. Drain thoroughly and sprinkle lightly with salt.
3. Place in a non-stick baking tray, without any fat, and bake in a preheated oven at 200°C, 400°F (Gas Mark 6) for 30–45 minutes or until soft in the centre when pierced with a fork.

DRY-ROAST POTATOES
SERVES 3–4
Cooking time: 1–1¼ hours
Oven: 200°C, 400°F (Gas Mark 6)

450–600 g (1–1¼ lb) medium-sized potatoes
Salt

1. Peel the potatoes and cut into even-sized pieces if you wish. Place in a pan of cold salted water, bring to the boil and blanch for 5 minutes.
2. Drain thoroughly then lightly scratch the surface of each potato with a fork and sprinkle lightly with salt.
3. Place in a non-stick baking tray, without any fat, and bake in a preheated oven at 200°C, 400°F (Gas Mark 6) for about 1–1¼ hours.

OVEN CHIPS
SERVES 4
Cooking time: 35–45 minutes
Oven: 220°C, 425°F (Gas Mark 7)

2–3 large, old potatoes
1 teaspoon oil

1. Peel the potatoes and cut into chips. Blanch in boiling salted water for 5 minutes. Drain well.
2. Meanwhile, pour the oil on to a baking sheet and place in a preheated oven at 220°C, 425°F (Gas Mark 7) for 7–10 minutes until the oil is very hot.
3. Spread the chips over the baking tray and turn them gently so that they are lightly coated with oil.
4. Bake for 35–45 minutes (depending on the size of the chips), until they are soft in the middle and crisp on the outside. Turn them once or twice during the cooking time.

One of the greatest delights of those following the Hip and Thigh Diet is the freedom to eat unlimited amounts of potatoes. Until now, chips have been strictly forbidden, but here is a recipe which widens still further the amazing versatility of this diet.

HIP AND THIGH DUCHESS POTATOES
SERVES 3–5
makes 6–10
Cooking time:
Boiling 20 minutes
Baking 15–20 minutes
Oven: 220°C, 425°F (Gas Mark 7)

450–750 g (1–1 ½ lb) old potatoes
2–3 tablespoons natural low-fat yogurt
A pinch freshly ground nutmeg
Salt
Freshly ground black pepper
A few drops oil

1. Peel the potatoes and cut into even-sized pieces. Place in a pan of boiling salted water and cook for about 20 minutes until tender. Drain well.
2. Mash the potatoes until smooth or pass them through a vegetable mill. Moisten with sufficient yogurt to soften them but make sure that they are still firm enough to hold their shape when piped out. Season to taste with a pinch of freshly ground nutmeg, salt and freshly ground black pepper.
3. Lightly brush a non-stick baking sheet with the oil. Spoon the potato mixture into a piping bag with a 1 cm (½ inch) rosette nozzle. Pipe into large beehive shapes and bake in a preheated oven at 220°C, 425°F (Gas Mark 7) for 15–20 minutes until lightly coloured.
4. Using a non-scratch spatula or palette knife, carefully remove from the baking sheet. Arrange on a hot serving dish or use as a garnish.

POTATO AND ONION BAKE
SERVES 4–6
Cooking time: 1–1 ¼ hours
Oven: 200°C, 400°F (Gas Mark 6)

450–750 g (1–1 ½ lb) old potatoes
175–225 g (6–8 oz) onions
300 ml (10 fl oz) vegetable or chicken stock
Salt
Freshly ground black pepper
A little low-fat spread (Maintenance Dieters only)

1. Peel and thinly slice the potatoes and onions. The attachment on a food processor or mixer is ideal because the vegetables will cook more quickly if they are thinly and evenly sliced.
2. Heat the stock and cook the onions in it for 3–4 minutes.
3. Place a layer of potatoes in the base of an ovenproof dish. Using a slotted spoon, remove the onions from the stock and place them on top of the potatoes. Cover with the remainder of the potatoes. Season each layer lightly with salt and freshly ground black pepper.
4. Pour the remaining stock over the potatoes, cover with a lid or aluminium foil and bake in a preheated oven at 200°C, 400°F (Gas Mark 6) for 1–1 ¼ hours until the vegetables are tender. Check them once or twice while they are cooking and press down so that the top layer is kept moist. Maintenance dieters can brush a little low-fat spread over the top. Uncover for the last 20 minutes of the cooking time so that the potatoes turn golden-brown on top.

STEAMING VEGETABLES

Prepare the vegetables in the normal way and place them in a steamer. Season lightly; experience will soon tell you how much seasoning is needed. The following cooking times are approximate; the actual times will depend on the age and size of the vegetables. If you wish, you can cook several vegetables in the same steamer, adding them at intervals according to the cooking time.

Vegetables	Cooking time (in minutes)
Broccoli	15
Brussels sprouts (small)	15
Carrots (old, in batons or slices)	20
Carrots (new, baby)	12–15
Cauliflower (florets)	10–15
Celery (2.5 cm (1 inch) slices)	15–20
Courgettes (batons or slices)	10–12
Leeks (small)	15–20
Mange-tout	7–10
Marrows (rings or dice)	10–15
Potatoes	20–30
Spinach	10–15

Seafood Salad (p. 52), Tomato and Kiwi Salad (p. 86), St Clement's Fool (p. 102)

SKINNING TOMATOES

Make sure that the tomatoes are ripe. Using the point of a small sharp knife, remove the cores. Plunge the tomatoes into boiling water for 30 seconds, then immediately transfer them to cold water and leave to stand until completely cold. This will prevent the flesh of the tomatoes becoming mushy.

TOMATO PASSATA

I discovered tomato passata many years ago in Italy and was delighted when I found it on the shelf of my local supermarket. It comes in bottles or cartons (like UHT milk) and is sometimes called 'creamed tomatoes'. In fact it consists of sieved tomatoes and is much thicker than tomato juice. However it is a liquid and not a paste like tomato purée.

I use tomato passata constantly as I find it thickens a casserole more readily than canned tomatoes and I prefer the taste. If you don't want to use a full bottle or carton, you can store the remainder in the refrigerator for five to six days, or freeze it for another time.

Roast Pork with Apricots (p. 67), Potato and Onion Bake (p. 95), Honey Yogurt Fool (p. 102)

SWEETS

Trying to find a luscious sweet made without cream can be very restricting and frustrating. This chapter should provide the answer to your problems. Light fluffy mousses, simple fruit sweets, chestnut meringues or an ice, all made with low-fat fromage frais or yogurt. Your friends and family will never believe you are on a diet when you give them these desserts. Because they are so low in fat, all the recipes can be eaten by Hip and Thigh Dieters at dinnertime.

SWEETS

Fruit Brûlé   100

Prunes in Orange Pekoe Tea   100

Spiced Plums   101

Fruity Rum Compote   101

St Clement's Fool   102

Honey Yogurt Fool   102

Mango and Orange Mousse   103

Loganberry Mousse   104

Baked Apples with Apricots (*Pommes Bonne Femme à l'Abricots*)   105

Raspberry Fluff   105

Pears Aurora (*Poires à l'Aurore*)   106

Peach Ambrosia   106

Raspberry Yogurt Ice   107

Red Fruit Ring   108

Oaty Yogurt Dessert   108

Chestnut Meringues (*Chamonix*)   109

FRUIT BRÛLÉ
SERVES 4

Any assortment of fruit can be used for this sweet. Oranges, grapes and apples form a good base; pears, plums, raspberries, strawberries and redcurrants all provide a contrast in flavour and texture. Even in winter a few frozen raspberries can be used but frozen strawberries are not recommended as they are too moist.

450 g (1 lb) prepared fruit
1–2 tablespoons lemon juice
450 g (1 lb) low-fat fromage frais or yogurt
4–5 tablespoons demerara or palm sugar

1. Using a small serrated knife, peel the oranges and cut out the segments. Wash the grapes, cut them in half and remove the pips. Peel, core and dice apples and pears. Remove the stones from plums and cut into pieces. Wash and pick raspberries, strawberries and redcurrants. Toss the apples and pears in the lemon juice. Drain all the fruit well so that it is quite dry.
2. Place the fruit in a heatproof dish and chill.
3. Preheat the grill until it is very hot. Just before you place the dish under the grill, spread the fromage frais over the fruit and sprinkle the sugar over the top. (It is important that this is done immediately before grilling, otherwise the sugar melts and does not caramelise.) Place the dish as high under the grill as possible and watch it all the time to see that it caramelises evenly. Turn the dish, if necessary, and take care that the sugar doesn't burn.
4. Allow to cool, then chill before serving.

PRUNES IN ORANGE PEKOE TEA
SERVES 4
Soaking time: overnight
Cooking time: 8–10 minutes

225 g (8 oz) prunes
600 ml (1 pint) cold Orange Pekoe tea
200 ml (7 fl oz) low-fat natural yogurt
1–2 tablespoons clear honey (optional)
Grated zest of 1 orange

1. Soak the prunes in the Orange Pekoe tea overnight. Then simmer them gently in the tea until tender.
2. Place the prunes in individual dishes with a little of the tea. Leave until cold.
3. Mix the yogurt with the honey (if used), and spoon a little on to each dish of prunes.
4. Sprinkle a little grated orange zest over the top of each. Refrigerate until served.

Mrs J. P. N. wrote:

'As you will see from this questionnaire, I could hardly be described as "overweight" being 7 st 9 lbs (49 kg) to begin with. However, I did have pads of fat on my hips which looked like saddlebags which developed during my last pregnancy, over fourteen years ago. I had found this fat impossible to shift, even after practically starving myself at one stage – all I succeeded in losing at that time was my bust! So, when I heard about the Hip and Thigh Diet I decided to give it a go, although I was very sceptical that it would work. You can imagine how I felt when I could almost literally see this very unwanted fat disappearing in front of my eyes. I am delighted with the results.'

SPICED PLUMS
SERVES 3–4

450 g (1 lb) large red or Victoria plums
1 orange
1 × 5 cm (2 inches) piece of cinnamon stick
2–3 cloves
Honey, sugar or artificial sweetener to taste
3–4 tablespoons low-fat fromage frais or 150 ml
*   (5 fl oz) low-fat natural yogurt*

1. Wash the plums, cut them in half and remove the stones. With a potato peeler, cut the peel very thinly from the orange. Then squeeze the juice.
2. Place the plums in a shallow pan with the orange peel and juice, the cinnamon stick and the cloves. Add honey or sugar to taste. Add sufficient water to the pan to poach the plums.
3. Cook the plums gently until tender. Then remove the orange peel, cinnamon stick and cloves. Add sweetener to taste if used. Chill.
4. Serve in individual glasses with fromage frais or yogurt.

FRUITY RUM COMPOTE
SERVES 4–6

2 oranges
1 small pineapple
225 g (8 oz) fresh cherries
225 g (8 oz) fresh apricots
300 ml (10 fl oz) natural pineapple juice
2–3 tablespoons rum or to taste
2 bananas

1. With a potato peeler, cut the peel very thinly from one of the oranges, making certain that there is no pith on it as this will be bitter. Cut into very thin strips and blanch in boiling water for 2–3 minutes until tender. Drain, place under cold running water until cold, then drain well again. Chill and reserve.
2. Using a small serrated knife, remove the peel and pith from both oranges and slice thinly. Cut each slice in quarters.
3. Remove the skin from the pineapple and slice into rings. Cut the core from each slice, then cut the slices into five or six pieces.
4. Wash and stone the cherries and apricots. Cut each apricot into four or five pieces.
5. Place all the fruit in a bowl with the pineapple juice and rum. Cover and refrigerate until served.
6. Just before serving, peel and slice the bananas and stir into the bowl of fruit, then sprinkle the strips of orange peel over the top.

St Clement's Fool
SERVES 4

1 × 11 g (½ oz) packet powdered gelatine (page 116)
5 oranges
1 lemon
450 g (1 lb) low-fat fromage frais or yogurt
50–75 g (2–3 oz) caster sugar or artificial sweetener to taste

1. Place the gelatine in a small bowl with 2 tablespoons water and leave to soften.
2. With a potato peeler, cut the peel very thinly from one of the oranges, making certain that there is no pith on it as this will be bitter. Cut into very thin strips and blanch in boiling water for 2–3 minutes until tender. Drain well and chill under cold running water, then drain well again and reserve. Using a small serrated knife, remove the pith from this orange and cut out the orange segments from between the membranes. Do this over a plate so that any juice is kept.
3. Grate the zest of another orange and the lemon. Squeeze the juice from all the oranges and the lemon.
4. Mix the fruit juices and grated zest together, then stir in the fromage frais, a little at a time. Add caster sugar or sweetener to taste.
5. Stand the bowl containing the gelatine over a small pan of hot water and stir until the gelatine has dissolved. Cool slightly, then stir into the fromage frais mixture, and leave in a cool place until it starts to set. Stir occasionally to mix in any gelatine or juices which may have sunk to the bottom.
6. When the mixture is on the point of setting, pour into individual glasses. Refrigerate until set, then decorate with the orange segments and sprinkle the strips of orange peel over the top. Serve chilled.

Honey Yogurt Fool
SERVES 4–6
Soaking time: overnight

Maintenance Dieters, if they wish, can use Greek strained yogurt for this sweet as it is thicker than ordinary yogurt. Make certain you choose the sheep's milk yogurt as it has less fat than that made from cow's milk. Hip and Thigh Dieters should use natural low-fat yogurt. This will give the fool a softer consistency but the result is still excellent.

Use a mixed packet of dried apricots, peaches, pears and apples but do not use prunes as they will discolour the sweet. (Dried fruit is easily obtainable from health food shops.)

The fruit can be puréed in a food processor or a liquidiser. If you use a liquidiser, it may be necessary to do it in two batches. A food processor gives a rougher texture which I prefer. For a really smooth purée, stew the fruit very gently for a few minutes until tender, then purée in a liquidiser.

225 g (8 oz) dried fruit salad (see introduction)
1 large banana
1–2 tablespoons lemon juice
1–2 tablespoons clear honey
225 g (8 oz) yogurt (see introduction)
3–4 extra dried apricots (do not soak)
A small piece angelica

1. Soak the dried fruit in cold water overnight. Then, if you prefer a very smooth purée, stew gently until tender. Drain the fruit, reserving the liquid which can be used in fruit salads.
2. Peel and slice the banana and place in a food processor or liquidiser with the fruit, lemon juice and about 1 tablespoon honey. Purée until smooth and transfer to a bowl.
3. Fold in the yogurt, taste and add more honey if you wish. Mix well and spoon into individual dishes.

4. Chop the extra dried apricots, place a few pieces in the centre of each dish and decorate with leaves cut from the angelica. Serve chilled.

MANGO AND ORANGE MOUSSE
SERVES 4–5

2 large oranges
1 × 11 g (½ oz) packet powdered gelatine (page 116)
1 ripe mango or 1 × 425 g (15 oz) can sliced mangoes
225 g (8 oz) low-fat fromage frais or yogurt
1 tablespoon lemon juice
Caster sugar or artificial sweetener to taste (optional)
A pinch freshly ground nutmeg
2 egg whites, optional (see right)

1. With a potato peeler, pare the peel very thinly from one of the oranges, making certain that there is no pith on it as this will be bitter. Cut into very thin strips and blanch in boiling water for 2–3 minutes until tender. Drain well and chill under cold running water, then drain well again and reserve. Grate the zest from the other orange.
2. Place the gelatine in a small bowl with 2 tablespoons water and leave to soften.
3. Using a small serrated knife, remove any remaining peel and the pith from both oranges and cut out the segments from between the membranes. Do this over a plate so that any juice is kept. Squeeze out any juice from the core.
4. Peel the fresh mango (if used) and remove the stone. Drain the canned mangoes if these are used. Discard the mango juice. Cut the fresh or canned mango into several pieces.
5. Place the mango and the orange segments (including any orange juice) in a food processor or liquidiser and puree until smooth. Pour into a large bowl.

6. Stand the bowl containing the gelatine over a small pan of hot water and stir until the gelatine has dissolved. Mix into the fruit purée.
7. Leave the mixture to cool, then stir in the fromage frais a little at a time, together with the lemon juice and grated orange rind. Add a little caster sugar or artificial sweetener to taste if you wish, and the freshly ground nutmeg.
8. Stir the mixture occasionally and when it starts to thicken, whisk the egg whites in a clean dry bowl until they stand in stiff peaks. Using a metal spoon or spatula, carefully fold the egg whites into the fruit mixture.
9. Pour into a bowl or individual dishes and refrigerate until set.
10. Sprinkle a few strips of orange peel over the centre of each dish just before serving.

If you prefer to avoid the use of uncooked egg whites, follow this procedure.

Omit the egg whites. Leave the fruit, gelatine and fromage frais mixture until it is on the point of setting then whisk vigorously with a balloon whisk or an electric whisk until the mixture is frothy. Pour into a bowl or individual glasses and refrigerate. Decorate as recipe. These mousses are best eaten the same day as they are made as they become rather firm if left overnight.

LOGANBERRY MOUSSE
SERVES 4

If you wish to save time or make the sweet when loganberries are not in season, use a 275 g (10 oz) can of loganberries. Fresh, frozen and canned raspberries can be used instead.

350 g (12 oz) loganberries
50 g (2 oz) caster sugar or artificial sweetener to taste
1 × 11 g (½ oz) packet powdered gelatine (page 116)
225 g (8 oz) low-fat fromage frais or yogurt
2 egg whites, optional (see right)
Frosted mint leaves (see right)

1. Wash and drain the loganberries.
2. Place the fruit in a pan with 4 tablespoons water and the sugar. Bring to the boil and simmer until tender. Allow to cool, then add sweetener (if used) to taste.
3. Rub the fruit (and juice from canned loganberries) through a nylon sieve until only the pips remain. (It is important to use a nylon sieve – a metal one would discolour the fruit.)
4. Meanwhile, place the gelatine in a small bowl with 2 tablespoons water and leave to soften. When it has softened, stand the bowl over a small pan of hot water and stir until the gelatine has dissolved. Mix into the fruit purée.
5. Stir in about two-thirds of the fromage frais, a little at a time. Mix well.
6. Stir the mixture occasionally, and when it starts to thicken, whisk the egg whites in a clean dry bowl until they stand in stiff peaks. Using a metal spoon or spatula, carefully fold the egg whites into the fruit mixture.
7. Spoon into individual glasses and refrigerate until set.
8. Meanwhile, make the frosted mint leaves.
9. Spoon the remaining fromage frais over the top and refrigerate until served. Decorate each glass with a few frosted mint leaves before serving.

FROSTED MINT LEAVES

These decorative mint leaves can be made several days in advance. They should be stored in an airtight container when dry and must not be refrigerated.

A few small sprigs mint
A little egg white
Caster sugar

1. Wash the fresh mint and drain until dry.
2. Whisk the egg white until it is frothy. Dip the sprigs of mint into the egg white and, if you wish, use a small paintbrush to coat the undersides of the leaves. Shake the excess egg white off the mint, then dust with caster sugar. Leave to dry on greaseproof or silicone paper. Use as desired.

If you prefer to avoid the use of uncooked egg whites, follow this procedure.

Omit the egg whites. Leave the fruit, gelatine and fromage frais mixture until it is on the point of setting then whisk vigorously with a balloon whisk or an electric whisk until the mixture is frothy. Pour into a bowl or individual glasses and refrigerate. Decorate as recipe. These mousses are best eaten the same day as they are made as they become rather firm if left overnight.

BAKED APPLES WITH APRICOTS
POMMES BONNE FEMME À L'ABRICOTS
SERVES 4
Cooking time: 30–45 minutes
Oven: 200°C, 400°F (Gas Mark 6)

Dessert apples, such as Golden Delicious or Russets, are best for this dish as they will keep their shape while being baked. If you prefer to use cooking apples, watch them carefully to see that they don't collapse. You may need to add more sugar or sweetener and adjust the cooking time.

12–16 dried apricots
2 tablespoons caster sugar, or artificial sweetener to taste
2 tablespoons rum
4 large dessert apples
1–2 tablespoons lemon juice
1 quantity Apricot Sauce (page 112)

1. Wash the apricots and cut into small pieces. Place in a bowl with 1 teaspoon sugar and the rum. Leave to stand for 1 hour.
2. Peel the apples, leaving the stalks in place. Cut a slice (or lid) off the top of each apple and reserve. Using an apple corer or a small sharp knife, core the apples and place in an ovenproof dish.
3. Using a slotted spoon, lift the prepared apricots out of the rum and divide them between the four apples. Place the apricots in the centre of each apple and replace the lids. Brush with the lemon juice and pour over the rum from the apricots. Sprinkle 1 teaspoon sugar (if used) over the top of each apple. Pour 150 ml (5 fl oz) water into the dish.
4. Bake in a preheated oven at 200°C, 400°F (Gas Mark 6) for 30–45 minutes. The apples must be cooked through but take care that they don't fall apart. Halfway through the cooking time, baste them with the juice and sprinkle a little more sugar or sweetener on each.

5. Meanwhile, make the Apricot Sauce (page 112).
6. Heat the sauce, pour a little over each apple and serve the rest of the sauce separately.

RASPBERRY FLUFF
SERVES 4

225 g (8 oz) fresh or frozen raspberries
1 egg white, optional (see below)
450 g (1 lb) low-fat fromage frais or low-fat yogurt
Caster sugar (optional)

1. Wash the fresh raspberries and drain well. Reserve a few for decoration and mash the rest slightly with a fork.
2. Whisk the egg white in a clean dry bowl until it stands in stiff peaks. Using a metal spoon or spatula, carefully fold into the fromage frais.
3. Layer the fromage frais and raspberries into four tall glasses, ending with a layer of fromage frais.
4. Decorate the top with a few whole raspberries. Refrigerate until required and serve with caster sugar if you wish.

If you prefer to avoid the use of uncooked egg whites, omit them and just layer the fromage frais and raspberries.

PEARS AURORA
POIRES À L'AURORE
SERVES 4
Cooking time: 20 minutes or more (depending on the ripeness of the pears)

Comice pears are best for this sweet as they have a nice round fat shape. Williams can be used but, like Conference, may need the stalk end trimmed and rounded to give them a good shape. This is best done before cooking. Tinned pears can be used for convenience.

4 ripe pears
2 tablespoons granulated sugar
1 × 5 cm (2 inches) piece of cinnamon stick (optional)
75 g (3 oz) glacé fruits, including ginger
225 g (8 oz) plain, low-fat quark or low-fat soft cheese (M, see p. 117)
225 g (8 oz) fresh or frozen raspberries
Icing sugar or artificial sweetener to taste
3/4 teaspoon arrowroot

1. Peel the pears, cut them in half and remove the stalks. Scoop out the cores with a teaspoon or melon baller.
2. Heat the granulated sugar and 450 ml (15 fl oz) water with the cinnamon stick (if used) in a frying pan with a lid. Stir until the sugar has dissolved.
3. Add the pears, cover and simmer very gently until translucent. Turn them once or twice so that they cook evenly.
4. When the pears are cooked, use a slotted spoon to lift them out of the pan and place them on a plate, cut side down, until cold. When the syrup is cold, pour it into a covered container. It will keep for about a week in the refrigerator and can be used for fruit salads.
5. Chop the glacé fruits and mix into the quark.
6. Divide the quark mixture between the eight pear halves, piling it up in the centre of each one. Place the pears cut side down in a serving dish.

7. Press the raspberries through a nylon sieve until only the seeds remain. (It is important to use a nylon sieve – a metal one would discolour the fruit.)
8. Add a little icing sugar to taste. If sweetener is used, add it after the purée has been thickened (see Step 9).
9. Place the purée in a pan and bring to the boil. Mix the arrowroot with a little water and add to the purée. Bring to the boil again, stirring all the time. Cook for a moment or two until the purée clears. Allow to cool slightly. Add the sweetener (if used) and pour a little purée over each pear. Pour the remainder around the base of the pears. Refrigerate until served.

PEACH AMBROSIA
SERVES 4

This dish is very quick and easy to make but the peaches may discolour if left too long (even if brushed with lemon juice) so assemble the sweet just before the meal if possible. The quark mixture can be made and the strawberries halved in readiness.

2 large ripe peaches
1–2 tablespoons lemon juice
1 orange
225 g (8 oz) plain, low-fat quark or soft cheese (M, see p. 117)
2 tablespoons Grand Marnier, any other orange liqueur or orange juice
175–225 g (6–8 oz) small strawberries
Extra Grand Marnier or orange juice (optional)

1. Place the peaches in a bowl, cover with boiling water and leave to stand for 1–2 minutes. When the skins are loose, plunge into cold water for a few minutes to prevent the flesh from cooking. Remove the skin, cut the peaches in half and take out the stones. Brush with lemon juice.

2. Grate the zest from the orange and mix with the quark and Grand Marnier or orange juice.

3. Divide the quark mixture between the four peach halves. Spoon into the centre of each one, piling it up if necessary to use all the mixture. Place the peaches cut side down on individual dishes. It doesn't matter if a little of the quark mixture shows around the sides.

4. Wash, drain and cut the strawberries in half and arrange them, pointed end outwards, around the peaches. Pour a little extra Grand Marnier or orange juice over each peach, if you wish, and serve.

RASPBERRY YOGURT ICE
SERVES 4–5

225 g (8 oz) raspberries
Caster sugar or artificial sweetener to taste
    (optional)
2 egg whites, optional (see right)
300 ml (10 fl oz) low-fat raspberry yogurt
A small piece angelica
75–100 g (3–4 oz) extra raspberries (optional),
    for decoration

1. Chill a 600 ml (1 pint) china bowl in a freezer or the freezer compartment of a refrigerator.

2. Wash, drain and press the raspberries through a nylon sieve until only the seeds remain. (It is important to use a nylon sieve – a metal one would discolour the fruit.) Or mash them with a fork. Add caster sugar or sweetener to taste, if you wish.

3. Whisk the egg whites in a clean dry bowl until they stand in stiff peaks.

4. Place the yogurt in a bowl and carefully fold in the egg whites, using a metal spoon or spatula.

5. Spoon one-third of the mixture into the base of the chilled bowl. Cover with half the raspberry purée. Repeat and finish with a layer of yogurt mixture. Cover well and freeze overnight until solid.

6. To serve, lightly moisten a plate. Dip a knife in hot water and run it round the side of the bowl to free the ice-cream. Turn out into the centre of the plate and slide into the centre if necessary. Decorate the base with the whole raspberries and small leaves cut from the angelica.

7. For the best results, place the ice-cream in the refrigerator for about 15 minutes to allow it to soften slightly before serving.

If you prefer to avoid the use of uncooked egg whites, follow this procedure.

Omit the egg whites. Soften and dissolve 1 teaspoon gelatine in 2 tablespoons water. Add to the yogurt with 1½ teaspoons glycerine. Mix well and place in the freezing compartment of a refrigerator or in a deep freeze until the mixture starts to freeze. Beat well with an electric whisk until smooth. Repeat 2 or 3 times until the ice crystals have broken down and the ice is smooth. Add the raspberry purée in the same way as the recipe, or, if you prefer, freeze the ice and pour the purée over just before serving. Allow the ice to defrost in a refrigerator for 15 minutes before serving.

RED FRUIT RING
SERVES 6

Any selection of red fruit can be used in this sweet and frozen fruit is also quite suitable. If redcurrants are not available use extra blackcurrants and raspberries instead.

75 g (3 oz) blackcurrants
75 g (3 oz) redcurrants
75 g (3 oz) caster sugar
7 level teaspoons powdered gelatine
75 g (3 oz) raspberries
I orange
I lemon
225 g (8 oz) low-fat cottage cheese
*225 g (8 oz) plain, low-fat quark or low-fat
    natural yogurt*
2 egg whites, optional (see right)

1. Pick the blackcurrants and redcurrants if necessary. Wash, drain and place in a pan with 1 tablespoon caster sugar and 150 ml (5 fl oz) water. Cook gently for 5–6 minutes until the fruit is tender but still holds its shape.
2. Meanwhile, mix 2½ level teaspoons gelatine in a small bowl with 2 tablespoons water. Leave to soften, then add to the fruit and stir until the gelatine has dissolved. Allow to cool slightly, then stir in the raspberries.
3. When the mixture starts to set, pour into a 1 litre (1¾ pint) ring mould and refrigerate until set. This layer must set before the next one is added.
4. Grate the zest and squeeze the juice from the orange and lemon.
5. Place the grated zest and juice in a food processor or liquidiser, together with the cottage cheese and quark.
6. Soften and dissolve the remaining gelatine in the usual way and add to the cheese. Purée until smooth. Add the remaining caster sugar.
7. Transfer the cheese mixture to a bowl. When it begins to set, whisk the egg whites in a clean dry bowl until they stand in stiff peaks.

Using a metal spoon or spatula, carefully fold into the cheese mixture. Pour into the ring mould and refrigerate until set.
8. To serve, lightly moisten a round plate and turn out the mould. Slide into the centre if necessary. Refrigerate until served.

If you prefer to avoid the use of uncooked egg whites omit them from the cheese layer and reduce the amount of gelatine in this layer to 4 teaspoons. Eat the same day as it is made.

OATY YOGURT DESSERT
SERVES 4

2 dessert apples
50 g (2 oz) seedless raisins
300 ml (10 fl oz) low-fat natural yogurt
4 tablespoons porridge oats
2 tablespoons golden syrup or honey
4 glacé cherries
A small piece angelica

1. Peel, core and finely chop the apples. Coarsely chop the raisins.
2. Place the yogurt in a bowl with the apples, raisins, porridge oats and golden syrup or honey. Mix thoroughly.
3. Spoon into individual glasses, cover with cling-film and refrigerate for 3–4 hours.
4. Decorate each one with a glacé cherry and leaves cut from the angelica. Serve chilled.

CHESTNUT MERINGUES

CHAMONIX
Makes 10–12
Cooking time: 2–3 hours
Oven: 110°C, 225°F (Gas Mark ¼)

This sweet is a variation of the larger rich and creamy *'Mont Blanc aux Marrons'* which was created by Escoffier. It is named after the small town of Chamonix which lies in the shadow of Mont Blanc. Fromage frais or yogurt is used instead of cream and I find either combines very well with the sweetness of the chestnut purée and meringue.

Make certain that you buy a small tin of *sweetened* chestnut purée (*'Purée de Marrons Glacé'*) and not the larger tins of unsweetened purée. The tins of sweetened purée most usually seen in the UK have blue and brown writing on them while the unsweetened ones have green. The sweetened purée is also available in tubes.

The meringue discs can be made well in advance, stored in an airtight container and used as required. Excess chestnut purée can be stored in a sealed plastic container in the refrigerator for a week or two.

The quantities given in the recipe are for decorating all the meringues but you can adjust the amounts and make as many as you need at one time.

2 egg whites
100 g (4 oz) caster sugar
A little icing sugar
1 × 225 g (8 oz) can sweetened chestnut purée
*4–5 tablespoons low-fat fromage frais or soft cheese (**M**, see p. 117)*
A little grated chocolate (Maintenance Dieters only)

1. Cover two or three baking sheets with silicone paper.
2. Whisk the egg whites in a clean dry bowl until they stand in stiff peaks.
3. Add 1 tablespoon caster sugar and continue to whisk until the mixture is stiff again.
4. Sift in half the remaining caster sugar and partially fold it in with a metal spoon or spatula. Then sift in the rest of the sugar and carefully fold it all into the egg white.
5. Spoon the meringue into a piping bag with a plain 1 cm (½ inch) nozzle. Pipe into 5 cm (2 inch) discs. Dust with a little icing sugar.
6. Bake in a very slow preheated oven at 110°C, 225°F (Gas Mark ¼) for 2–3 hours until dry. When they are cooked, remove from the oven, lift them off the silicone paper and place on a wire rack until cold. Store in an airtight container.
7. Spoon the chestnut purée into a piping bag with a plain 3 mm (⅛ inch) nozzle and pipe a nest around the edge of each meringue. Just before serving, spoon a little fromage frais into the centre of each one. Maintenance Dieters, if they wish, can sprinkle a little grated chocolate over the top.

Joanne Goulding wrote:

'I just thought that I would write and tell you how successful your Hip and Thigh Diet has been for me and to express my thanks to you for developing it.

As I was not really overweight or fat to start with I was quite amazed that I lost weight and in the right places.'

Joanne lost 1 in (2.5 cm) from her bust and waist, 3 ins (7.5 cm) from her hips, 3½ ins (9 cm) from her widest part, 2½ ins (6 cm) from each thigh and 2½ ins (6 cm) from around the top of each knee. At 5 ft 1½ ins (1.56 m) she was delighted to reduce from 8 st 7 lbs (54 kg) to 7 st 12 lbs (50 kg) – ideal for her height.

SAUCES

Sauces are an essential part of cooking as they add colour, flavour and interest to so many dishes. In many cases, the sauce is part of the recipe but in some instances they are made separately and, most of the time, can be made in advance. These are the recipes given in this section.

The Sweet and Sour Sauce (page 113) is very quick to make and is better made each time you need it. But to save time, why not make larger quantities of the other cooked sauces and freeze the extra for another occasion?

SAUCES

Oil-free Vinaigrette   112

Apricot Sauce   112

Piquant Plum Sauce   112

Sweet and Sour Sauce   113

Tomato Sauce   113

OIL-FREE VINAIGRETTE
Makes 200 ml (7 fl oz)

I find it convenient to make this amount of dressing and store it in the refrigerator ready for use when needed.

150 ml (5 fl oz) red or white wine vinegar or cider
    vinegar
50 ml (2 fl oz) lemon juice
1/2 teaspoon salt
1/2 teaspoon freshly ground black pepper
3–4 teaspoons caster sugar
1 1/2 teaspoons French mustard
Chopped fresh herbs such as thyme, marjoram,
    basil or parsley (optional) or 1 crushed clove
    garlic or 1/2 teaspoon garlic paste

1. Mix all the ingredients together. Pour into an airtight container (e.g. a jar with a tight-fitting lid) and shake well. Taste and add more salt, black pepper or sugar if you wish.
2. Store in the refrigerator and shake well before using.

APRICOT SAUCE
SERVES 4–6
makes 300–450 ml (10–15 fl oz)
Cooking time: 15–20 minutes

225 g (8 oz) dried apricots or 1 × 400 g (14 oz)
    can apricots in natural juice
Caster sugar or artificial sweetener to taste
2–3 tablespoons rum (optional)

1. Wash the dried apricots, place in a bowl, cover with cold water and soak overnight.
2. Place the apricots in a pan with 200 ml (7 fl oz) of the water in which they were soaked. Cook over a gentle heat until tender.
3. Purée the stewed or tinned apricots with their juice in a food processor or liquidiser until

smooth. Add the sugar or artificial sweetener to taste. Stir in the rum, if used.
4. Serve hot or cold.

PIQUANT PLUM SAUCE
SERVES 4
makes about 300 ml (10 fl oz)
Cooking time: 25–30 minutes

This delicious sauce can be served with gammon, duck and pork and could also be eaten as a pickle with cold meats.

350 g (12 oz) dark red plums
1 medium-sized onion
A pinch chilli powder
1/4 teaspoon ground ginger
1/4 teaspoon ground allspice
100 ml (3 1/2 fl oz) malt vinegar
65 ml (2 1/2 fl oz) water
120 g (4 1/2 oz) soft light-brown sugar

1. Wash and stone the plums. Peel and chop the onion. Place in a pan with the spices, malt vinegar and 65 ml (2 1/2 fl oz) water. Simmer gently, uncovered, for about 20 minutes until the plum skins and onion are tender.
2. Purée the plums in a food processor or liquidiser or through a vegetable mill.
3. Return to the pan, add the sugar and stir over a gentle heat until the sugar dissolves. Then bring to the boil and boil rapidly, uncovered, for 7–10 minutes until the sauce thickens. Remove from the heat and leave until required.

*Red Fruit Ring (p. 108) Oaty Yogurt Dressing
(p. 108), Chestnut Meringues (p. 109)*

SWEET AND SOUR SAUCE
SERVES 4
makes 150–200 ml (7 fl oz)
Cooking time: 1–2 minutes

This tasty sauce can be served with all varieties of firm white fish. It is also very good with chicken and pork. Prepare the onion well in advance so that the juice is ready when you need it. However, if you are short of time, a finely grated onion can be used instead.

1 small onion
2 teaspoons caster sugar
1 tablespoon tomato purée
1 tablespoon soy sauce
1 tablespoon white wine vinegar or cider vinegar
1 tablespoon honey
Juice of 1 lemon
Juice of 1 orange
Freshly ground black pepper

1. Prepare the onion 1–2 hours before it is needed. Peel and thinly slice the onion. Place the slices against the sides of a soup bowl or similar dish. Sprinkle over the caster sugar and leave to stand for at least 1 hour for the juice to form.
2. Mix all the ingredients with the onion juice (not including the onion slices) in a small pan. Bring to the boil and cook, uncovered, for 1–2 minutes. Use as required.

TOMATO SAUCE
SERVES 4–6
makes about 300 ml (10 fl oz)
Cooking time: 25–30 minutes

This sauce is quickly made and freezes well so you may wish to make several quantities at once.

If you prefer a very smooth sauce, use 300 ml (10 fl oz) tomato passata (page 96) instead of canned tomatoes. When the sauce is cooked, purée it in a food processor or liquidiser or through a vegetable mill. Then add stock or water according to the recipe (Step 4).

1 medium-sized onion
1–2 cloves garlic or 1/2–1 teaspoon garlic paste
1 × 400 g (14 oz) can chopped tomatoes
Salt
Freshly ground black pepper
A good pinch granulated sugar
1 teaspoon lemon juice
Vegetable stock or water as necessary

1. Peel the onion and fresh garlic. Finely chop the onion and crush the garlic.
2. Place the onion and garlic in a pan with the tomatoes (including their juice). Season lightly with salt and freshly ground black pepper, and add the sugar and lemon juice.
3. Bring to the boil and simmer gently, uncovered, for 25–30 minutes until the onion is tender.
4. Check the seasoning, adding more salt, pepper, sugar or lemon juice as required. Dilute the sauce with stock or water, if necessary, to give a pouring consistency.

Baked Apple with Apricots (p. 105), Spiced Plums (p. 101), Prunes in Orange Pekoe Tea (p. 100)

FACTS AND FIGURES

One or two of the cooking techniques and ingredients used in this book need a little explanation so to prevent constant repetition they have all been gathered into this section. A chart is also included to show at a glance which foods are high or low in fat content. This will help you to select ingredients carefully when producing your own recipes.

Dry-frying

Frying is often an important part of a recipe as it seals the juices in the meat and gives added flavour and colour. For anyone on the Hip and Thigh Diet, dry-frying is the ideal way to do this as no fat is used.

You will need a heavy-based pan. Make certain it is really hot before you begin cooking. Test the temperature with one piece of meat. It should seal the outside immediately. If the pan is not hot enough, the juices will seep out and the result will be tough, colourless meat.

For the same reason, do not overload the pan with meat. Cook it in several batches. Too much turning or stirring will cool the meat and the juices will run out. This applies particularly to mince, so make sure the meat is sealed and browned well on the bottom before you turn it. If any fat runs out (this is most likely to happen with mince), pour it away. Add the stock or wine and, with a wooden spatula, mix in any juices which have caramelized in the pan so that this extra colour and flavour is not wasted.

Grillades

These are heavy cast-iron pans with a ridged surface. They provide a different method of grilling and are very suitable for Hip and Thigh Dieters. Most meats and offal can be cooked on a grillade. Thick whole fish, such as trout, or thick cuts of fish are ideal but whole or filleted plaice and sole are better cooked under a conventional grill. Boned chicken and duck breasts can be cooked on a grillade but it is not suitable for other poultry joints, petits poussins and kebabs. They should be cooked under a normal grill, on a barbecue or in the oven.

Gelatine

Gelatine comes in 11 g sachets. For convenience, I have converted this as ½ oz but in fact it is a little less. The amount in one sachet is equivalent to 3 level 5 ml spoons (teaspoons).

Fromage Frais

Fromage frais is used frequently in this book. It consists of skimmed milk and lactic acids and is made with two different fat contents. The low-fat variety has only 0.1 per cent fat and one grocery chain states that 'it is virtually fat-free'. The other fromage frais has cream added to it and has a fat content of 8 per cent. Only the low-fat fromage frais should be used in the recipes in this book.

Fromage frais is a delightful accompaniment to fresh fruit instead of cream. If you find it rather sharp for your taste, sweeten it with a little sugar or liquid artificial sweetener.

Take care when using fromage frais in sauces. Heat it gently; it must not boil as it will curdle if overheated. For this reason, sauces are best made on the cooker, not in a microwave. Low-fat yogurt can be substituted for fromage frais, although it should be used carefully in cooking as it may curdle when heated.

Quark

Quark is a soft cheese which comes from Germany. It is made with skimmed milk and has a fat content of less than 1 per cent. Other low-fat soft cheeses should not be used by Hip and Thigh Dieters as they have a higher fat content. Until recently the plain, low-fat quark was the only one available but I have noticed a new, medium-fat, flavoured quark which has a fat content of 12 per cent. Do take care to use only the plain, low-fat variety. If quark is not available you can substitute other low-fat cheeses, but these should only be eaten by Maintenance Dieters when marked with an **M**.

Fat Values of Dairy Products

	Fat per 100g
Yogurt	
Low fat natural	1.1%
strained Greek ewe's	6%
strained Greek cow's	10%
Cottage cheese	
half fat	1.5%
Fromage frais	
ordinary	8%
low fat	0.1%
Quark	less than 1%
Other low fat soft cheeses	8%

Grams per 25g/1oz (approx)

Food	1	2	3	4	5	6	7	8	9	10	11	12	13	14	15	16	17	18	19	20	21	22	23	24	25

Alcohol — ◆

Beans
- Baked — ◆
- Kidney — ◆

Biscuits
- Sweet — ~5
- Savoury — ~4
- Rye — ~1

Bread — ~1.5

Breakfast Cereal
- Muesli type — ~3
- Porridge (dry) — ~2.5
- Flakes – Corn or Bran — ~1
- Weetabix — ~1

Butter & Butter Substitutes
- Butter — ~20
- Flora — ~20
- Low Fat Spread — ~10.5
- Gold Lowest — ~6.5

Cakes
- Cakes – Average — ~5.5
- Pastry – Average — ~8.5

Cheese
- Ordinary Cheddar — ~8.5
- Low Fat Brands — ~4.5
- Cream Cheese — ~12.5
- Low Fat Soft Cheese — ~2.5
- Fromage Frais — ~1
- Low Fat Fromage Frais — ◆
- Cottage Cheese — ◆
- Quark - Low Fat — ◆

◆ = negligible

Grams per 25g/1oz (approx)

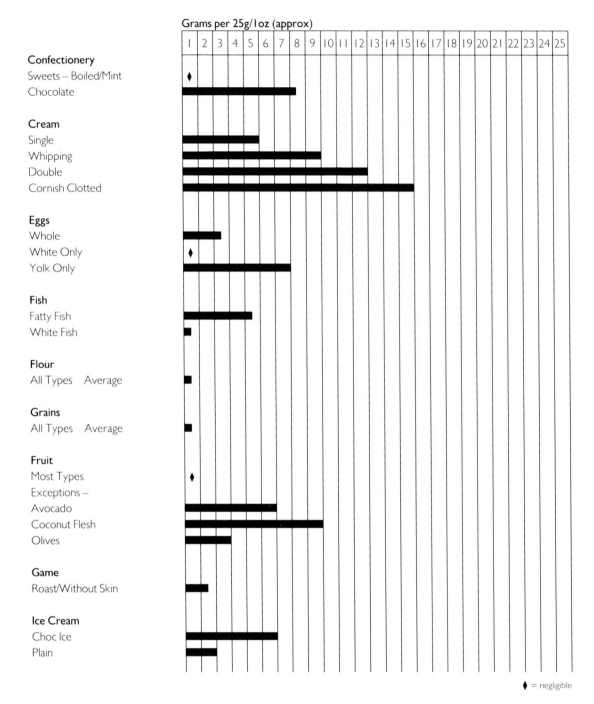

♦ = negligible

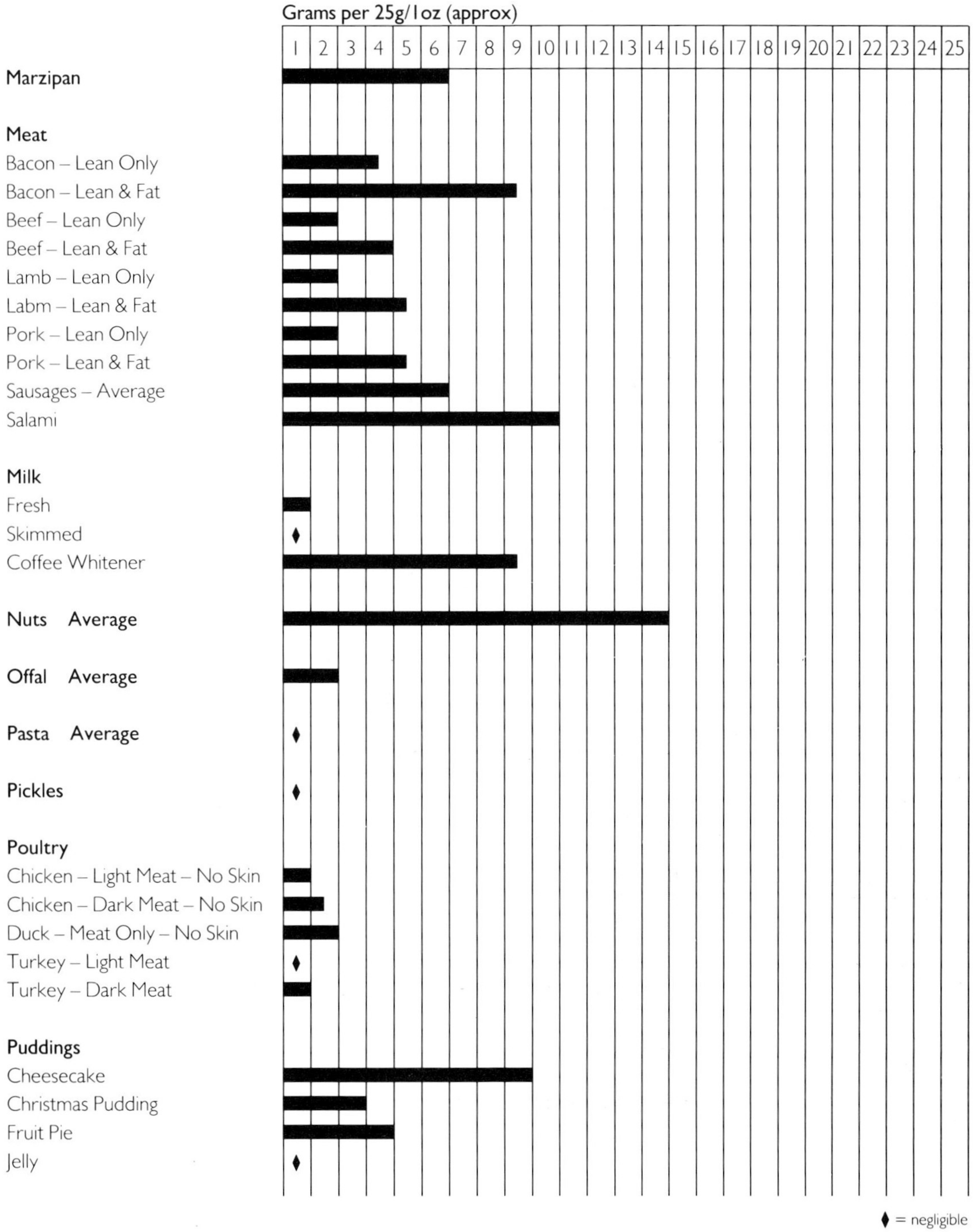

Grams per 25g/1oz (approx)

	1	2	3	4	5	6	7	8	9	10	11	12	13	14	15	16	17	18	19	20	21	22	23	24	25

Marzipan

Meat
Bacon – Lean Only
Bacon – Lean & Fat
Beef – Lean Only
Beef – Lean & Fat
Lamb – Lean Only
Labm – Lean & Fat
Pork – Lean Only
Pork – Lean & Fat
Sausages – Average
Salami

Milk
Fresh
Skimmed
Coffee Whitener

Nuts   Average

Offal   Average

Pasta   Average

Pickles

Poultry
Chicken – Light Meat – No Skin
Chicken – Dark Meat – No Skin
Duck – Meat Only – No Skin
Turkey – Light Meat
Turkey – Dark Meat

Puddings
Cheesecake
Christmas Pudding
Fruit Pie
Jelly

♦ = negligible

Grams per 25g/1oz (approx)

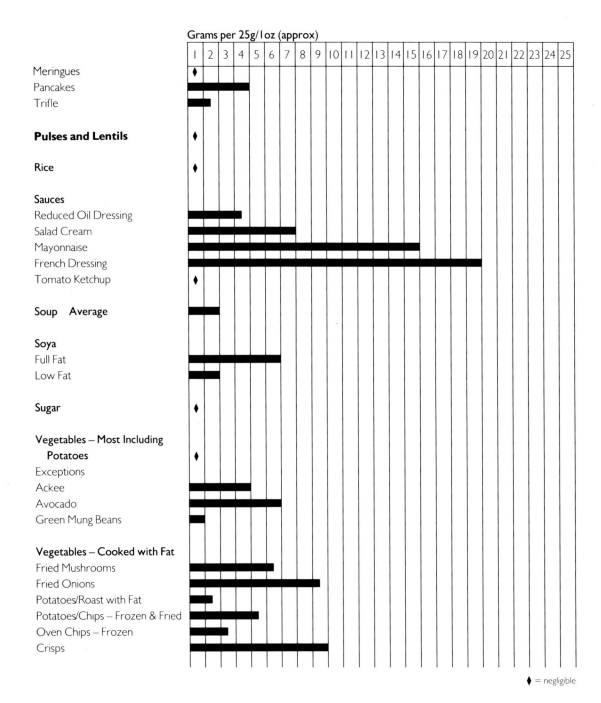

	1	2	3	4	5	6	7	8	9	10	11	12	13	14	15	16	17	18	19	20	21	22	23	24	25

Meringues
Pancakes
Trifle

Pulses and Lentils

Rice

Sauces
Reduced Oil Dressing
Salad Cream
Mayonnaise
French Dressing
Tomato Ketchup

Soup   Average

Soya
Full Fat
Low Fat

Sugar

**Vegetables – Most Including
   Potatoes**
Exceptions
Ackee
Avocado
Green Mung Beans

Vegetables – Cooked with Fat
Fried Mushrooms
Fried Onions
Potatoes/Roast with Fat
Potatoes/Chips – Frozen & Fried
Oven Chips – Frozen
Crisps

♦ = negligible

Grams per 25g/1oz (approx)

	1	2	3	4	5	6	7	8	9	10	11	12	13	14	15	16	17	18	19	20	21	22	23	24	25

Yoghurt
Most Low Fat Brands ♦
French Style Set Yogurt ♦

Yorkshire Pudding ▬

♦ = negligible

INDEX